Call Me Elizabeth

Call Me Elizabeth

DAWN ANNANDALE

with MARY ALEXANDER

TIME WARNER
BOOKS

TIME WARNER BOOKS

First published in Great Britain in April 2005
by Time Warner Books

A CIP catalogue record for this book
is available from the British Library.

ISBN 0 316 72976 0

Typeset in Berkeley by M Rules
Printed and bound in Great Britain
by Clays Ltd, St Ives plc

Time Warner Books
An imprint of
Time Warner Book Group UK
Brettenham House
Lancaster Place
London WC2E 7EN

www.twbg.co.uk

For the people I love and to those who had faith.
Michael, always.

Acknowledgements

So many people have supported, encouraged and loved me throughout this whole experience; to you all I say thank you, which seems so inadequate, but thank you all so much for your belief in me.

Mary, for caring enough to listen, to really listen and to feel.

Rebecca, for your vision, patience and Kleenex. I still have your umbrella.

Sharon and Kerry for encouraging me to do this in the first place. For the buckets of tears, the bottles of wine and the late-night phone calls. For your friendship I will be forever grateful.

Woo and Gramps: if I could choose my parents it would be you two. (Aren't you lucky!!) Thank you Lois and Steve for keeping me in touch with reality.

John and Debbie for your opinions when asked, and for never judging.

Rod and Mr Upchurch the bailiff – for your trust.

To the team at Time Warner, especially Jo and Sheena-Margot, who must be sick of the sight of this book by now!

Christine Comyn for your beautiful art work on the cover of this book. They say a picture speaks a thousand words. Your picture conveys my feelings to perfection.

Thank you all.

Prologue

*I*t was lunchtime on a Monday, and I could hardly believe what I was thinking of doing. I was sitting at my desk eating my sandwich, with a free magazine, *Ms London*, lying in my lap. It was open at the job ads. But what did I want with a job? I already had a full-time position as a legal secretary. But still my eyes kept flicking back to one particular advert.

Attractive girls required for escort work. Earn up to £300 per night. Phone——

I flipped the magazine shut and took another bite of my chicken salad sandwich. I chewed it automatically, tasting nothing as my thoughts raced. How could it have come to this? How could I, thirtysomething years old, married with six kids aged between two and twelve and a nice home, even be contemplating answering an ad for escort girls? After all, any fool knew what the ad really meant. This advert was about sex. It might not specifically say so, but it didn't have to. Everyone knew 'escort' was a euphemism for 'prostitute'.

I sat back in my chair, frowning as I tried to understand what half my brain seemed to be urging me to do. Was I seriously considering having sex with strangers for cash? Were things really that bad?

Yes. They were.

To an outsider, my life looked steady, secure, perhaps even enviable. I lived in Kent in a big house in a good neighbourhood; my children were well-dressed at all times. My elder kids were privately educated, while the younger ones spent the weekdays with their much-loved childminder. My husband Paul worked in the successful family building firm, while I had a good job in London. My children did a round of after-school activities from horse-riding to singing. Our life was a privileged, middle-class existence.

But the truth that underlay this storybook tale of happiness was that our outgoings far exceeded our income, and had done for some time. Six children don't make life cheap, and on top of this Paul and I were very probably guilty of trying to live a champagne lifestyle on an orange juice budget. After years spent living in denial, our debts had now risen to such a tottering pile that they threatened to bring down our entire way of life. We were on the brink of losing everything.

For months I'd battled to make ends meet, doing the best I

could with the money we had, paying the most essential bills first: school fees, or the kids couldn't go; the car payments, or that would be taken back. The less essential bills, always red, were pushed to the back of the kitchen drawer as I tried not to panic. I hardly dared to ask myself how much longer this could go on. But a week ago, I'd had the answer to this question forced on me: the bailiffs had called. This time, it had been a warning, but in two weeks they'd be back, and then, they'd said, they'd take things. I knew they weren't joking.

Ever since, I'd been frantically trying to come up with a way to earn more money, and fast. I knew it was all down to me. My father was dead and my mother didn't speak to me. Paul wasn't able to help – he might work for the family firm, but he could not earn enough to bail us out. But how could I, a secretary earning £300 per week, turn our financial situation around? I rolled the problem over and over in my mind, never any nearer an answer. Nevertheless, I knew I had to find one. There had to be a way.

After the visit from the bailiffs, I had steeled myself to face our debts in full. I'd totted up all the bills and the amount we owed wasn't good news. The mortgage on the house was in serious arrears, and I hadn't managed to pay the council tax, gas, electricity or water bills for several months. The credit cards were up to the max, and I didn't even bother trying to get money from the hole in the wall. The debts were mountainous, but somehow, anyhow, I had to tackle them if we weren't to lose everything.

I took another bite of my sandwich and chewed dispiritedly as

I contemplated my rather limited range of options for the zillionth time: I could give up the house and move all the kids from their schools where they were so happy; win the lottery; rob a bank; or find a seriously good way of coming up with a large amount of money, fast.

My heart plummeted at the thought of the first option. My own childhood had involved endless changes of school, something which I'd hated and which had helped to mar my already difficult early years, leaving me with a sense of insecurity that had followed me into adulthood. I so didn't want to inflict that on my own children. And the house was our stability, our home. Surely that had to be the final thing to go? I desperately wanted to maintain my children's security, particularly with their father being increasingly erratic and unreliable.

The second and third options were so unlikely they didn't count. This left the final one as my only hope.

I opened the magazine again and looked at the advert for the umpteenth time. Was this two-liner my seriously good fourth option?

Suddenly, my mind was made up. I would do anything to safeguard my kids. And I meant *anything*. Before I lost my nerve, I was going to ring that number and get myself a well-paid night job that could save us all. I was going to become an escort girl.

This is a true story, although names and locations have been changed to protect people's identity. There are some aspects of my marriage to Paul that I have not been able to talk about in this book, as they are his story to tell and not mine. Writing it has not always been an easy task. I have had to face up to my life in all its colourful, messy detail, from some of the long-buried, terrible things that happened to me as a child to the implications and consequences of my decision to become an escort.

But on one point I am very clear: I don't regret becoming an escort. I did it because it seemed to me to be the only way to save my children from momentous physical and emotional upheaval at a time when they were already watching their parents' marriage fall apart. I had always wanted the fairy tale for my kids – the gingerbread cottage with the picket fence, and two happy parents waving the smiling children off to school. Now, with serious problems at home, I knew that wasn't going to happen for them. But while I couldn't save my marriage, I could prevent my children from losing the rest of their happy, familiar world: their schools, their friendships, their home. I became an escort so I could pay off our debts and maintain our stability.

I know the path I chose isn't for everyone; I'm well aware that prostitution is considered morally questionable by most of society. I also know first-hand that it's not an easy path to take. But for all its ghastliness – the endless sex with strangers, the prevalence of drugs, the risk of being raped, the outlandish things I was asked to do, the exhaustion, my marriage breaking down, the worry about the children while I was working – it was all, in my opinion, worth it, and I'd even do it again if I had to.

How can I be so sure? The proof is in the pudding: years later, my kids are happy, confident and stable.

So this is my story, told from the very start. Going back to the beginning, to my childhood, is important if you're really to understand, because my motivation to do anything – even to have sex with strangers to protect my children's happiness – was laid down early on in my life, in my own muddled, unhappy childhood, and in my fervent desire to give my kids what I didn't have – a happy, stable beginning.

Was I so wrong? Read on, and judge for yourself.

Chapter One

I was born in Chatham, Kent, in March 1967. My brother, Andrew, was a just over a year old then, and three years after my arrival came Richard and then Joanne. My parents were both hard-working and ambitious. My father was a marine engineer, while my mother stayed at home – somewhat reluctantly but on my father's instructions – and fulfilled the traditional role of home-maker, wife and mother.

At the start of their marriage, my mother, Rosemary, idolised my father and rarely, if ever, challenged his authority at home. It had not been an easy courtship – they had both gone against the wishes of their families by marrying – and my mother, particularly, had taken what was a fairly drastic step in those much more conservative times, for love.

Family history has it that Rosemary had always been a bit of a rebel, but even bearing this in mind, giving up everything for my father at the age of sixteen was a big thing to do. But that is exactly what she did. For love, she turned her back on her father, a lieutenant-colonel in the army, and her mother, who was from a wealthy land-owning family, walked away from the opportunity to go to university, and began a relationship with my father, William, a man from a different social class whom her parents disliked from the start.

William, despite his lean, dark good looks, was not at all what my maternal grandparents had hoped for for their attractive, red-haired eldest daughter. They had probably been thinking along the lines of a nice captain from a good local family, or at least a clever, smart young man from the professional classes. William didn't even begin to measure up to these hopes, as he was essentially a working-class boy in the process of making good. While my mother's childhood home was a large detached house on one of the best streets, William hailed from the back end of a council estate on the extreme fringes of the town, and he was just as far removed socially from Rosemary as he was residentially. William's father was a cook for the Royal Navy, and his mother worked as a shop assistant. William's parents called lunch dinner, and dinner tea, and had, as Rosemary reported back home with a kind of mock-horror, simply no idea how to hold a teacup.

Nevertheless, Rosemary was in love and, despite the obvious social differences, determined to be with William. This was a decision she underlined within months, by falling pregnant at seventeen. To my maternal grandparents, this was something that simply wasn't done – or if it was, every step was taken to conceal the fact.

These days, having a baby while unmarried doesn't raise so much as an eyebrow, but back then it was truly a scandal. These were the days when abortion was still illegal and wayward daughters were sent to unmarried mothers' homes to sit out their pregnancies unsupported, before handing over their babies to married couples who for some reason or other couldn't have children of their own.

A baby out of wedlock simply wasn't 'done' in my grandparents' circle, and they hated the fact that their daughter had embarrassed them so. Their social circle consisted of fellow army folk and the local gentry, with whom they had comfortable, unchallenging conversations, the wheels of which were oiled by sherry or gin and tonics, but Rosemary's pregnancy changed all that overnight. People started to gossip about Rosemary at my grandfather's regiment, conversations dwindled away to nothing as he approached, and he received too many embarrassed, pitying looks from acquaintances as the news quickly spread all over town. For my grandparents, it was all too much. They more or less washed their hands of my mum, and abandoned her to her choice. It wasn't that my grandparents were heartless – they were simply the products of their class and time.

There was equally little understanding from William's family. Why, they wondered, had their only son chosen this smart, rather distant woman with ways they didn't understand to be his girlfriend and mother to his children? Rosemary, in her turn, warmed to none of William's family.

9

So my parents came together against a background of disapproval, and their union meant the merging of two very different cultures without any support from either of the cultures they came from. In a way the odds were stacked against them from the start – theirs was always bound to be a marriage beset by frictions. But in the beginning, they didn't feel them. They loved each other, were young and healthy, and prepared to work hard. How bad could life be? It was the sixties, when new opportunities were opening up for everyone. They didn't worry about what people thought, and got on with the job of living their lives.

My parents married soon after I was born. As the scandal surrounding their early years together receded, and my father progressed speedily in his career as an engineer, to the outside world our life must have appeared to be a typically affluent and happy one. A prosperous father, a homemaking mother and four healthy, obedient children. But as in so many homes, the reality of life behind our closed front door was quite different.

Cracks in the marriage began to appear early on. My mother might have thrown in her lot with my father, but she hadn't intended to choose a life of unremitting domesticity. She was a talented artist, but her ambitions to paint were squashed by my father, who thought she was ridiculous and childish to harbour such notions. Her job, in his opinion – and that was always the only opinion that counted in our household, as she was fast learning – was to run the home. It was his job to be the provider. Their roles were clearly defined, by him, and he didn't want any crossing-over or confusion. But my mother felt differently, and battled endlessly for her right to a life of her own. This was to be an issue throughout their marriage. The more my father fought to control my mother, the more she shouted back and struggled for some semblance of freedom.

These tensions exaggerated and distorted qualities that already existed in both my parents. For my father, having a wife from a social class that he viewed as superior to his own meant that he had signed up for a lifelong inferiority complex. To cope with this, he was always trying to prove his worth, and so, a determined man – he had put himself through night school to get his degree in engineering – he became a driven one. A strong-willed man, he became, over time, a ferocious and controlling bully.

In my mother's case, it was her rebellious nature that had led her to choose my father as her husband, but now he wanted to contain her more than her own parents, with their conservative ways, had ever done. Her frustrations at having her world made so small and rigid crystallised into a bitterness that would colour every aspect of her life. And these qualities – his bullying, her bitterness – weren't just reserved for each other. They spilled over into the lives of us four children, too, and came to dominate our childhood.

In the early days of their marriage, when I was a toddler, we emigrated to New Zealand and settled in Wellington in the North Island. So many families had already made the leap to either Canada or Australasia in the sixties that I don't think our departure was considered to be out of the ordinary – the British economy was faltering and many families were looking for new opportunities. Hydroelectric power was developing rapidly and providing jobs for able technicians such as my father. I remember it as a wildly exciting time for all of us – my dad would never have had such a chance if we had stayed in England. He found work at the gas turbine plants between the islands, a fascinating and well-paid job that allowed him to make use of his skills as a marine engineer. For my mother it was harder: she had to manage four small children in an unfamiliar environment far away from her friends. What I remember – I was a very small child at that time – was the relative freedom and luxury of it all. Nothing seemed too difficult or too challenging, and home life wasn't yet too unhappy.

My father was, as I've mentioned, very determined. He was a man who reckoned he could do anything. He was ambitious for himself and wanted the best for us – he set himself goals and then went flat-out for them until he achieved them. He went to evening classes to learn how to fly a plane, so he could take us on trips in a light aircraft. He took a course in architecture so he could design and build a house for us, which he then proceeded to do. He was incredibly capable, my dad, and talented; able to achieve whatever goal he set himself through sheer application and force of will.

But he was also restless – achieving a goal didn't satisfy him for long. Instead, he'd move straight on to the next challenge. It was this restlessness that meant that four years later we were on our way back to Kent, for good. My father had joined the Merchant Navy as a chief engineer, and the four of us were sent to a small private school for children whose parents were in the forces. Aged just nine, I found the atmosphere warm and nurturing, and I quickly settled and made friends. But it was to be a short-lived happiness. The restlessness struck again, and when I was ten we moved once more, this time back to the town where both my parents had come from.

The move meant leaving everything I knew and at this stage it mattered. It meant saying goodbye to my friends; it meant a new school, a new house, a new beginning. My parents were excited, but I dreaded it. However, unavoidably, the day of the move came. It seemed to me that our old life had been packed away and now stood about our empty home in tea chests. Trying not to get under the grown-ups' feet, I watched silently, clutching one of my favourite treasures – a music box with a lady inside it seated on a red velvet chair – as several men loaded all our possessions into a large white van, pausing in their efforts only to drink cups of tea proffered by my mother. Finally, we climbed into the car and followed the van.

It was something of a triumphant return for my parents. The new house was a big, detached house on the smartest street in town. It had an in-and-out gravelled drive and vast gardens. A huge magnolia tree dominated the front of the house, while an aged laburnum stood at the back. Built in the 1930s, the house had four large bedrooms, a sitting room, dining room, lounge and conservatory.

For my father, who had begun life in a council house on an estate on the outskirts of town, the ownership of this house meant he had really arrived. For my mother, the colonel's daughter who had married beneath her, it was as if she had come back to her roots. She was delighted to find herself once again in material circumstances equivalent to those she had been born in. She now had the trappings to go with the grand social status that she had always maintained. She wasted no time and began to settle in immediately.

The house was furnished with things purchased by my parents from various parts of the world they had spent time in. In the conservatory there was a vast sheepskin, made of several fleeces stitched together, from our New Zealand days. The wooden dining-room table and chairs came from India, where my father had worked the previous year, as did the intricately carved coffee table in the sitting room. A huge rug of pink and gold dominated the lounge. The overall effect was rich and warm. But none of this warmth was reflected in the family atmosphere. My mother was determined that the house should look perfect at all times, not an easy task with four kids. She shooed us out of doors as much as possible, leaving her free to polish and clean and plump up cushions. We all quickly realised the value she placed on neatness, took off our shoes whenever we dared to venture inside and generally took care not to make a mess.

All obviously mess-creating activities were outlawed: there was no art, no sticking and pasting, no cooking unless we were helping Mother prepare a family meal; no muddy boots inside, no food except at the kitchen table. There were rules for everything. My childhood home looked the part, but it certainly didn't ring with the laughter of four children happy at play; rather it was a still, hushed place that instinctively made me want to talk in a whisper, to creep into the corners of its big, impressive rooms, almost to disappear. Increasingly, that seemed to my ten-year-old self to be the easiest way to keep out of trouble.

My sister Joanne, just six, and I shared a bedroom, furnished with twin beds with cotton counterpanes, a large wooden chest of drawers, a bookcase and a television. I tentatively set about personalising my area. I stuck up my Pierrot poster on one wall, and sat the various dolls I had collected and my beloved music box on top of the wooden chest. Reading filled much of my spare time, and books quickly began to fill the shelves of the bookcase. I read widely and passionately, willing to try almost anything. Enid Blyton's Famous Five series stood shoulder to shoulder in the bookcase with books on Greek mythology. That first autumn, as I struggled to make friends at my new, large school with its endless corridors that all looked confusingly the same, and to keep out of my increasingly angry mother's way, I read to escape, to visit another life, somebody else's life, perhaps a life I might find easier than my own. For those hours that I lay on my bed turning page after page, I almost was George in the Famous Five adventures, or one of the twins at St Clare's. I wept for Persephone separated from her lover and banished to the underworld for part of every year, and read and reread the joyous reunion at the end of *The Railway Children*.

But books could only take me so far away from reality. Too often, I had to live in the real world, my world, and face everything that meant. My mother had always ruled us children with a firm hand. She had not forgotten the standards of her own childhood in terms of behaviour, and she applied them to us in turn. She didn't want her children growing up unable to use the correct knife and fork, wherever their father might have come from. So while our friends might live on TV dinners, we sat down to supper at the properly laid table as a family every evening.

She constantly corrected our manners until they almost became instinctive. Perhaps she felt it was something she could bring to the family, something she had to offer which my father, with his different background, didn't; or perhaps it was a way of reminding him that in some things, however much he bullied her, she simply knew better. She grew increasingly strict with us. There were no kisses or hugs or bedtime stories, nothing of any warmth, that was simply not her maternal style.

With hindsight I see that she was unhappy. Certainly she seemed to hate me and take out her frustrations with life on me, definitely more than the other three children. I think it was because she was becoming ever more angry at my father's desire to control her and she had to take it out on someone. The years had passed, she had achieved nothing of her artistic dreams, and it was as if she finally realised – and resented – what she had given up for him, and hated him for it. The constant tension that hung in the air was frequently punctuated by shouting matches as she fought for her freedom. Even at the age of ten I could see it was a battle my mother wasn't going to win. My mother might be strong-willed, but my father ran the household and everyone who lived there. We kids all knew that.

My father never hit my mother (as far as I am aware), but verbally he could be very cruel and cutting in a way that would be viewed as emotionally abusive today. He told my mother which friends she could see, what evening events she was allowed out to – the school report evenings were approved of and therefore allowed, while outings with friends he didn't like were not – and how she could spend her spare time. He controlled her friendships, getting rid of anyone he didn't like by creating a scene. My mother's best friend, Fiona, was one of his early victims.

Rosemary and Fiona had been best friends since their school days. For years Fiona had tolerated William only because he was my mother's husband, although she'd never liked him or the way he tried to control Rosemary. At the same time, my father had never given Fiona any reason to like him, being rude and unfriendly to her whenever she visited, and continually running the friendship down to my mother.

However, Fiona had held on to her friend through thick and thin – until it came to the last straw. My father was working on a job in Bangladesh, and wrote to my mother claiming that Fiona had written to him to tell him that Rosemary was having an affair. All parties knew this was simply untrue, and that there had never been such a letter (as my father finally admitted years later, when it was too late to resuscitate the friendship), but for Fiona and her husband it was all just a step too far. They knew William was controlling and dominating, but now he was casting his vicious net more widely by lying about them. They'd simply had enough. My mother, for her part, was so worn down by my father that she didn't have the strength any more to fight for the friendship. The two women quietly gave up on it.

Our friends from school and elsewhere would often undergo similarly awful treatment at the hands of my father. I remember my brother Andrew became friendly with an Indian boy he'd met at school. This prompted William to reveal his racist side with a series of barbed remarks that were supposed to be 'jokes' when Andrew's friend came for tea one day. Needless to say, the boy didn't seek Andrew out in the playground any more, let alone come to visit him at home again. All of us silently absorbed the message of this incident: don't bring friends home.

The loss of such friendships, both our own and our mother's, meant our world became a very small one, and deprived us all of regular social contact. Fiona had been a happy, normalising presence whenever she had visited us, and we missed her. With two children of her own, she used to bring her own brand of joy with her whenever she came. She would call me darling and give me a kiss, and I would wonder how this lovely, warm person could be best friends with my mother, who was so hard and bitter. Somehow Fiona conveyed to me that she knew my father was a monster, and my mother totally dominated by him, and offered silent understanding and a hug.

That kind of glimpse of normality was essential to my survival, and planted the germ of longing for my own family, the family that I was one day to be willing to do anything to protect.

Fiona, through her behaviour to her own children, Amanda and Neil, showed me that my mother's brand of child-rearing wasn't the only kind. I remember observing how freely Fiona hugged and kissed her kids, and thinking, Why can't I have a bit of that kind of love? Amanda fell over and grazed her knee one day, and Fiona picked her up and kissed and cuddled her until she stopped crying. I remember watching this, practically open-mouthed, for in my experience when children grazed their knees, they were told to get up immediately and not make a fuss.

My grandpa, my mother's father, would visit occasionally if my father was away, and once in a while we would go and see him – always without my father, who refused to go. The chip on his shoulder, his inferiority complex, wouldn't allow him. It was as if he felt he could never cross to their world, so he wasn't even going to try, or let anyone see he was bothered. How Grandpa had a daughter like my mother made me stretch my childish eyes wide with wonder. Together we played hangman and boxes, and when that palled he would tell me stories about the war. He'd give me a stick of rhubarb from his garden and a saucer of sugar to dip it into. The few hours I spent with Grandpa were memorable – because I was happy.

Similarly, although my mother, snob that she was, couldn't cope with the social ways of my paternal grandparents, Grandad and Nanny showed us their own brand of fun and kindness. I remember happy games of indoor golf played in the entrance corridor of their house, which involved trying to hit oranges into teacups placed on their sides. They'd also feed me delicious foods my mother considered deeply unsuitable, like fried eggs and fried bread.

Such small pleasures and relationships punctuated the bleak emotional landscape that was my home life. What I didn't know was that far far worse was to come; my childhood was about to take a much darker turn.

My father's latest job took him to Libya, to work at a power plant. He was to be away from home for months on end – a six-month posting would be rewarded with a month's leave. His absence meant that at least the shouting stopped, although my mother clearly resented having to cope single-handedly with four children in his absence, and was even crosser with us children, me particularly, for that. Still, home was a slightly better place while my father was away.

It was on his first leave home that my relationship with my father changed irrevocably.

That first day of his return, all of us kids were leaping on him in excitement, jumping around and fighting in the lounge. However unpleasant he could be to us, he was still our dad, and I suppose it was our instinct to be pleased to see him. I remember I had on my favourite green trousers, flares, very trendy. Then I was sitting on his lap, and somehow we were alone together. He pushed my legs apart and started rubbing me through my trousers. I can still recall lying in bed that first night he was home, bewildered and scared, wondering what on earth had happened to the father who had left home six months before.

That was the first time. After that, he got into a pattern of touching me whenever he could. There were lots of 'accidental' brushings against me during the day, and at night he'd volunteer to read my bedtime story. My father would sit in the gap between the twin beds, reading a book to Joanne, while behind his back he would slide his hand under the duvet and start rubbing me down there. I lay there frozen. I couldn't speak. What was this? I didn't know. But I did know that it shouldn't be happening.

One morning, it got worse. My father came into my bedroom early one Sunday, woke me up with a finger on his lips to be quiet, and took me downstairs to the cloakroom. He locked us in, and then put his erection in my hands. He moved my hands up and down on it, and said, 'That's how you do it.' I remember thinking, What am I doing? and then all this stuff came out all over my hands. My stomach lurched and vomit rose in my throat. 'Don't tell anyone,' he ordered. 'They won't believe you.' Then my father sent me back to bed.

After that, there was no stopping him. He would tell my mother that I'd been naughty and was clearly too much for her to handle, so why didn't he keep me with him that day and spare her the trouble of me? Of course this multiplied his opportunities to touch me, and gradually he became bolder and bolder until one day he tried to have penetrative sex with me.

Everyone else was out, I don't remember where. My father took my clothes off, picked me up and put me on the kitchen worktop. He undid his flies, drew out his erection, and tried to push himself into me. He couldn't – I was just a little girl.

21

When it was over, I crept quietly upstairs. I had the bedroom to myself and I was glad I didn't have to explain what was wrong to anyone. I climbed into my bed and snuggled under the duvet, as though I was ill. I took down my music box and turned it on. I'd had the box since I was very small, and loved the tune – 'Für Elise'. As the music tinkled away, I stroked the red velvet that covered the chair the doll sat on. After a while, I pulled on a little piece of the red velvet, and a few threads came off in my hand. I pulled another piece and then another until a small white bald patch started to spread. I stared with horror at the white plastic revealed under the velvet. What had I done? Why was I destroying one of my most loved things? Confused, I put the box back down on the chest of drawers and lay down, my face hot against the cool of my pillow. I listened to the music mixing with the noise of the rain hitting against the windowpane. Gradually, the music box stopped. Still I didn't move. I was thinking, and yet trying not to think. Life seemed very complicated. Finally, a soothing blankness washed through me as I lay there, feeling very small and helpless in the face of the knowledge that it was only a matter of time until my father succeeded where he had failed today.

My father's failed attempt at penetration was just his first try. There were countless, countless times after that, so many I can't remember them all, or perhaps I have made myself forget. He'd make me help him in the greenhouse or the garage, so he could get me alone. He'd make me squat down, push my knickers aside and touch myself, or he'd lie on top of me and try and force his way in. I was never very cooperative, but, undeterred, he'd persevere while I lay beneath him as still and silent as a corpse. I never said a word. I knew there was no point in resisting or telling anyone. My father had made it quite clear that no one would believe me. I just had to put up with it.

I tried to cope with it as best I could. Each time it happened, I tried to shut it out, tried to distance myself from my body, to pretend it wasn't me. In my head I was elsewhere, I was reading my favourite book, or shooting the winning goal in a netball match, or over at a friend's house for tea. Anywhere but where I actually was, on the floor of the greenhouse or garage, with my plaits trailing in the dirt and my school skirt rucked up to my waist, my father lying on top of me, panting.

Each time, after it was over, I'd take refuge in my room with my books and my dolls and my beloved music box. A few weeks went by before I noticed that there was no red velvet left on the chair. In the despair and confusion that I wasn't able to begin to articulate, even if there had been anyone to tell, I had picked it all off.

Gradually, as weeks turned to months, I began to notice a pattern of behaviour emerging in my father. After each episode with me, the house would always be calmer for a day or two. My father wouldn't shout at my mother, or at us children, quite so much. It was as if abusing me calmed my father down. I didn't understand why this should be, but the realisation meant that I absorbed early in life a message that was, ironically, to reoccur on my future path in life: sex was something that was for the pleasure of other people, not for me. For me, it was something to be got through, to be endured, by thinking of something else until it was over.

My father held all the power and he knew it. As an adult, he was physically stronger and considered more believable than a little girl. Of course he told me over and over again not to tell anyone: 'If you tell anyone, you'll all go into care, and you don't want that for your brothers and sister, do you? Besides, no one would believe you anyway, you're such a little liar.' Not many episodes went by without that threat being repeated.

I never challenged his words. I was too afraid, and too helpless. But somewhere inside me, my childish instinct for right and wrong, though squashed, was not extinguished, and I knew what he was doing was wrong. Not only because he didn't want me to tell anyone, but also because he occasionally tried to justify his actions to me. I remember he once said: 'I'm doing this for you. So that when you are a big girl, you won't be shocked by the size of a man.'

Did my mother know what my father was doing to me? I've asked myself this question many times. The answer is, I don't think so. Certainly she seemed to resent the time he spent with me. She appeared jealous of the attention my father seemed to be lavishing on me, which I thought made her dislike me more than she already did. She did not stop my father from hitting me, his apparent favourite. On one occasion, he left such welts on my legs and bottom that they didn't send me to school for a couple of days. When I did finally go back, I showed my best friend Lorna the by now fading marks. She was horrified and immediately said she should tell her father, who was a GP. This of course horrified me in turn. I knew the beating, along with

24

the abuse, was a secret never to be told. In public, we remained a smart, happy family living on the best street in the town. I begged her not to. I even told her I'd been very naughty and deserved it. Eventually, reluctantly, she promised she wouldn't say anything.

Looking back on it, I see that my father deliberately drove a wedge between my mother and me to ensure I had nowhere to go when he abused me. He was forever moaning about me to her, and she would in turn regale family friends with my wrongdoings. They must have thought that I was a real pain, regardless of how I behaved, because, well, people believe adults, not kids, don't they?

Only once did I try to tell someone what was happening to me. I've always been closest to my eldest brother, Andrew. One day, when I was about twelve, we were in the tree house at the bottom of the garden. It was a damp autumn afternoon and already getting dark. I don't really recall what I told Andrew as I stared pointedly out at the laburnum tree, but I do remember Andrew saying, 'Don't be silly.' He didn't understand, and since I didn't really understand what I was trying to tell him, who could blame him? Then our mother called us in for tea and, embarrassed, as if I had done something wrong, I climbed down and trudged back up the garden, knowing that if Andrew didn't believe me, there was absolutely no one who could help me. I was trapped, unsafe in my own home, unable to leave; I had nowhere to go to avoid having sex with the one man a daughter should be able to count on for protection in life. My only hope was that I would outgrow the problem. I had to hurry up and grow up so I could leave home and move beyond my father's reach.

And so I began to wish my life away. The moment I was an adult and able to support myself, I could leave. I didn't care where I went; I couldn't get that far in the fantasy. I just wanted to be safe, to not be shouted at by my mother, or sexually abused by my father. In the meantime, I developed a kind of survival strategy. The aim was simple: to avoid my father as much as possible, and to get out of the house as often as I could.

Suddenly I was very keen on after-school clubs. I joined everything possible from needlework to swimming. I was in the netball team, which had several practices after school as well as matches and tournaments which took me out of the house at weekends. As soon as I was considered old enough, I took up a paper round, leaving home each morning at 6.30 a.m. This allowed me to breathe a little easier, as it meant that my father had to get up extremely early to have a chance to abuse me in the mornings, something that he largely didn't bother to do. I took on a typing course two evenings a week, and volunteered to be in the school play. I wasn't very good, but playing Mother Superior in *The Sound of Music* kept me out of the house on Wednesday evenings for a whole term, and that was the point.

As I got older, I filled Sundays with a job at the local Wimpy. I'd go round to my friends' houses whenever possible. Carol, Gillian and Mary, my three close friends, all lived nearby, but my mother didn't approve of them – perhaps as they lived in little terraced houses rather than a great house like ours. Nevertheless, I'd slip over there on a Saturday afternoon when I could. I couldn't go too often, because, lovely though their parents were, I felt embarrassed – they must have wondered why I never asked their daughters back.

I grew up some more, and Saturday nights out became an issue. Sometimes I'd be invited to sleep over with Gillian. Those Saturdays were good Saturdays: we would meet in town, browse in Dorothy Perkins, trying on ra-ra skirts before going on to Boots to experiment with make-up, and then go back to her house.

On most Saturday evenings, we would go out for a few hours. Gillian's parents would wave us off, reminding us to be back by ten-thirty, and we would set off to meet our little crowd in the local pub. It would usually be Gillian and me, our other girlfriends, and a few boys from the local grammar. We might have a beer, or see a movie. It was all very tame teenage stuff. Time and again, I found myself locking eyes with one boy in particular: a boy named Hal, son of a local headmaster. The strange unfurling feeling in my stomach told me that I liked him, and his smile told me he liked me back.

But even with my first boyfriend, my clubs, my sports activities, my jobs, wherever I was, the abuse was always with me, a sinking feeling in my stomach day and night. Whatever I was doing, wherever I was going, I was planning around my father. I didn't want to be alone with him, yet every night, after school and clubs had finished, I had to go home in the end. As I trudged along the pavement each night, my footsteps slowing the nearer I came to home, I'd hope against hope either that he was out or that my brothers, sister and mother were home too. The company of others offered me some protection, even the company of my mother.

And every now and then, oh bliss, it would be like someone had waved a magic wand: his work would call him away at short notice, and suddenly he'd be gone for a couple of months. Overnight I was free of the actual reality of him, even if the fear of his return stayed with me, niggling like a warning light that never went out in my mind. Even though I knew he'd be back, and that it was only a matter of time before he was cornering me somewhere once again, at least, for a while, he was gone.

By the age of sixteen I had achieved good O level results and was planning to take three A levels. I worked hard at school, knowing that my future rested entirely on me. I was sure I was going to make something of myself. With my passion for reading and writing, I had set an ambition early in life – I was going to be the editor of *The Times*.

But one morning I discovered that my parents had other plans for me. A few days after my O level results, I was sitting having breakfast with my parents. The sun was pouring in the window and bouncing off the parquet floor. I was about to make my excuses and get down when my mother told me that she didn't want me to go back to school after all. It was time I got a job. I stared at her for a moment, frowning. But, I stammered, I had just worked hard at my O levels in order to go on to further education. No, my mother said, shaking her head decisively. That wasn't going to happen. I was too difficult, she told me, to handful. Not, she went on, like Andrew, such a help, such a son. No, further education was not for me; I was to make my own way in the world as soon as possible. It seemed that I obviously didn't deserve the expenditure of further education.

I turned slowly to my father. Did he feel any differently? Apparently not. I was a girl, and further education would be wasted on me. I absorbed this message slowly. After years of not rocking the boat, of not making a scene, of never daring to put forward my opinion, of putting up with whatever my parents dished out, I felt I had no choice. It seemed I had to go along with their decision.

'All right,' I mumbled, fighting back tears. 'I'll start looking for a job.'

Hard though it was at first, I knew I had to be practical. I began to rearrange my dreams. I decided to apply for a position as a trainee buyer, and wrote to several department stores. I was quickly offered a job with Harrods, a store my mother approved of. It was an eighteen-month position, and would result in a BTEC national, a well-recognised qualification. And there was an advantage to giving up on my university dream: I knew that the sooner I was earning, the sooner I was free.

In the autumn of that year, while my friends put on their school uniform and went back to school for the sixth form, I joined the working world.

At first, I commuted to Knightsbridge. But as I made friends with the other girls at Harrods, I began to spend nights at their

if they didn't have a bed. 'Don't you

ald I begin to explain that the floor of

a more comfortable than the bed in my

rst pay cheque. And money meant freedom,

away from home as much as possible. Staying

wit.   came a habit. If I bought the food for supper, my

friends le.   stay with them. It was an arrangement that suited us

all, and my visits home dwindled to the minimum.

As I stayed in London more and more, working and having fun with my friends, I had a constant niggling feeling that I had forgotten to do something. I'd rack my brains for what it could be, but just couldn't put my finger on it. Finally, I realised what it was: I wasn't worrying about my father abusing me. Because he simply wasn't there. I didn't constantly have my guard up. It was a revelation. I'd lived with the abuse, and the fear of it, for so long that it had almost become a part of me. Now that I realised it was possible for me to live a safe, different life free of my father, I resolved that the moment I qualified and had a full wage to live on, I would properly leave home for good.

The day I left was one I'll always remember. I had finished my training period and passed my BTEC. This meant I was now going to earn enough money to rent a little place of my own. It was a late spring day, cold but with a clear blue sky, and I was nearly eighteen. I took the train from London and walked from the station in the direction of home, carrying an empty suitcase in my hand. I walked up the drive, the familiar curl of fear flooding through me, and let myself into the house. It was quiet, as still and menacing as I had remembered. I felt as if I could almost see the haze of misery that hung in the air. I'd never liked this house.

Years of training made me take my shoes off. Then, quietly, hoping no one was in, I climbed the stairs to my room and laid the suitcase down on the bed. I quickly packed up the last of my clothes and put my favourite books on the top. I added my music box, dear painted lady on her now-bald chair who had seen me through so much, and my best-loved dolls, and pulled down the lid. I lifted the suitcase off the bed and looked around.

This is the last time I will stand in this room, I thought, eyes lingering for a moment on the poster of the Pierrot and the one of Adam Ant, the subject of a youthful crush. I left without a backward glance.

I went back downstairs as quietly as I had gone up them, the suitcase light in my hand: the sum total of nearly eighteen years of living. I opened the front door and stepped out into the world again. Relief spread through me as I crunched out of that grand carriage drive for the last time.As the gravel gave way to the stone slabs of the pavement, I stood in the safety of the street and looked back at the grand old house that had been the scene of so much unhappiness. Suddenly, a light came on in my parents' bedroom. So someone had been in after all. My father? I shivered involuntarily in my warm woollen coat and turned resolutely in the direction of the station. Never, I told myself, would I intentionally sleep under my parents' roof again. As I turned the corner, my pace quickened, my mood lightened. Finally, I was free.

Leaving home marked the end of my childhood and the start of real life for me. But it wasn't until two years later that the family broke down completely. My father had been having an affair, something which I had known about for a while since his mistress, Alison, was the mother of a friend of mine. I'd kept this information to myself. I certainly wasn't going to say anything; who was I to rock the already rocky boat? But my mother's sister Fay felt differently. When she found out about the affair, she felt strongly that my mother should know, and rang her up and told her.

It was almost as if my mother had been waiting for the excuse. The very next day, she contacted the family lawyer and filed for divorce. My father immediately moved in with Alison. This made my mother incandescent with rage. It was the ultimate humiliation to have this out in the open, to have the whole of the town know that her husband William preferred Alison. It quickly became clear that the divorce was going to be as acrimonious as the marriage. But my father wasn't going to give in easily. He responded to my mother's aggressive divorce claim by demanding custody of Joanne and Richard, the two younger children, who were still under age.

My mother hit the roof. It was while she was sounding off about my father and the years she'd put up with him that Andrew unintentionally gave her the ammunition she needed to win not just the battle but the whole damned war. 'Mum,' he said, fed up after a litany of after-all-I've-had-to-put-up-withs, 'you weren't the only one who suffered, thanks to him. Think of Dawn. Think of what she went through at his hands. Count yourself lucky.' It seemed that Andrew *had* listened that day back in the tree house after all, and he hadn't forgotten. He had believed me, and now he couldn't live with the information any more. That night my mother didn't stop nagging him until he caved in and told her the whole story.

On learning how my father had abused me, my mother picked up the phone to the lawyer. 'Tell William,' she thundered to the lawyer, 'tell William that I'll tell the world how he sexually abused Dawn unless he drops the custody claim and gives me everything I ask for.'

Of course William agreed to Rosemary's divorce demands, and my mother thought she had won the last round. But she was wrong – there was one more tragic act to come. Before the divorce was finalised, my father killed himself, leaving no will. He gassed himself in his car, and by dying intestate before the divorce details were through, by law only half his estate went to my mother; the other half went to his four children.

My mother was furious, certain he had done it to thwart her. By committing suicide when he did, William had ensured that Rosemary received far less than she had expected under the divorce settlement.

Her response was immediate. She demanded 'her' money back from all of us children. The two boys, Richard and Andrew, obliged, although they promptly 'borrowed' it back. Joanne's was by law placed in a trust fund until she reached eighteen. And mine? I kept it. It wasn't much, but after all I'd been through, I didn't see why I should give it back. This was to be one more wedge between my mother and me, but there were so many by now that our relationship had become almost non-existent. While she barely spoke to me, to the outside world she seemed the perfect grieving widow. Outwardly she was a woman who had lost the man she loved, and was now left alone in the world to care for her four children. Behind closed doors it was a very different story. How appearances can deceive so absolutely – one of the lessons I had been learning for much of my childhood – was finally rammed home for good then, never to be unlearnt.

As for me, I didn't grieve for my father. A couple of days after he had died, I remember staring into my coffee cup, unable to stop myself looking back at my childhood. I had a picture in my mind of how we must have looked to the outside world: the big house with the immaculate front lawn, home to a happy brood of children, loving mother somewhere inside rustling up some nutritious dish for supper. It was a picture that I suddenly wanted to believe in. It was as if I wanted to romanticise it, deny its ghastliness; to indulge in the fantasy of how it could have been.

I shook my head and the fantasy was gone. 'There's no point in this,' I told myself sternly. 'You can't change the past. You can only look to the future.' And so I did.

I was only twenty but I already understood perfectly well that the only way I was going to have the family life I desperately wanted – the cosy one in the adverts with the kids bouncing around while their parents watch them, laughing fondly; the one with the fairy-tale start, middle and ending; the one featuring the loving mother at the top of the bill – was to begin one of my own.

Chapter Two

So there I was, twenty years old, all alone, and desperately insecure. I had no family but hated being on my own, so there was never a gap of more than a few days between boyfriends if I could manage it. Looking back with all the benefits of hindsight, I see that my insecurity then – hating being alone and wanting some wonderful man to look after me – coupled with my burning desire to create a warm family life meant that I was very vulnerable to trying to build my future with the wrong man.

I was looking for a man who would give me what I wanted – stability and children – and magically make my life all right. In old-fashioned terms I wanted a good provider, a decent, caring family man. Now that I'm older and wiser, I know that finding this kind of man requires a complex recipe of love, trust and commitment; and that many men find that kind of commitment rather terrifying, or after trying it for a while decide it's not for them. But back then, buoyed up by the optimism of extreme youth, I felt sure it was simply a matter of meeting the right man and off we'd go into the sunset on his white charger and into the Happily Ever After.

Then, I met a man who seemed to have some promise in this direction. Robert, twelve years older than me, was a member of the Young Conservatives Association, where I was serving as secretary of the South-East area. We started going out. Friends have asked me how I found it possible to embark so easily on a romantic and sexual life after what happened to me at the hands of my father. But I had so compartmentalised the abuse that it didn't occur to me to feel apprehensive about trusting Robert, or having sex with him. The experience with my father didn't seem related in any way to the experience of falling in love, with all that that entails. It was truly like I was doing something completely different, that I'd never done before. I thought I loved Robert, I certainly found him attractive. I felt as I suppose most young women do when they meet someone and fall a little in love.

But the relationship was to be a short-lived affair. Within weeks I was pregnant, and when I broke the news of my pregnancy, Robert's potential as the provider and family man evaporated in front of my eyes. He simply couldn't cope with the idea of a child. Horror-struck by the turn of events, he retreated rapidly and the relationship was over as quickly as it had begun.

Although it sounds a nightmarish situation – early twenties, no family, and pregnant with no partner in sight – I only remember that I simply got on with life as it unfolded. I don't recall being heartbroken at Robert's desertion; only how much I looked forward to having the baby, even if I was going to be a single parent – after all, this was the beginnings of the family I was yearning for. Even if circumstances weren't quite ideal, they weren't that bad either. I had my little house, my job – I'd left Harrods by now and had started working as a secretary in London – and a good circle of friends.

My friends were all excited for me, and kept buying me babygros that looked impossibly small, barely larger than my hand. Could a baby really start out that size? I hung some red curtains in the spare room, and bought a pram which stood, expectant, in the hall. At night I would lie in my bed feeling the baby kick, and wonder about the relationship we would have, this child and I. Of one thing I was certain: my child was going to have a very different life from my own. Together we'd splash in puddles and make Playdoh creations and glittery craft pictures and to hell with the mess. My child's home would be a warm place where his or her friends were always welcome.

I was looking forward to motherhood. I was young, but I knew we'd manage. It felt really exciting to think of 'we', not just me. I planned to find a childminder when the baby was born, so I could continue to work and support us both. I had it all straight in my head, and, somehow, none of it fazed me. I just had the energy and optimism that you have at that age, coupled with the new sense of freedom at living life as I wanted to live it, far far away from the shouting and screaming that had dominated my childhood. This was still such a novelty that it made all of life rather enjoyable.

Knowing I wasn't going to be yelled at, or worse, for the slightest unpredictable thing made life seem so light, the smallest things so pleasurable. And I was relishing it. If I wanted to take my shoes off in the middle of the hall and leave them there all night, I could. If I wanted to sit with my feet curled up under me on the sofa, or change channels to a programme of my choice, or dance round the room to my favourite Abba song, no one was going to yell at me for doing it.

Then, just when I'd got used to the idea of facing the pregnancy alone, I met someone else. Could this be Mr Right? I certainly hoped so.

Peter was ten years older than me, which, despite my experience with Robert, for some reason still gave me an automatic sense of confidence in him from the start, as if by being older he just had to be wiser as well. We had met years before in the local pub when he had had an evening job there, and we became reacquainted in similar circumstances. Peter worked for an electronics company and, encouraged by my rather feverish nesting instincts, soon moved in with me.

Since Peter was older, he suggested that he look after all the finances, and I happily agreed. It was all rather amazing. Here at last was someone to look after me! We bought a house together, and Peter arranged the mortgage. He ran the joint account, so every month I just paid in my salary cheque and left him to pay all the bills.

Emily was born, I was smitten, and Peter was sweet with her. He supported me while I stayed at home with Emily for her early months and during this time asked me to marry him. I didn't have to think hard about it before saying yes. This wasn't the great romantic love I'd read of as a child – he was no Mr Darcy, nor was I Elizabeth Bennet – but it seemed to have all the ingredients I required. Peter was a kind, mature man willing to build a family life, which was what I wanted above all else. I had already seen that he had the makings of a good father from his behaviour with Emily, and if we were married he would be, to all intents and purposes, her dad. My daughter would have a father, and my family life would be settled, just as I'd always hoped. How could I turn him down?

So Peter and I were married, and he adopted Emily. No sooner had I gone back to work, leaving Emily, now nearly one, with a childminder, than I fell pregnant with my second child. There I was, in my early twenties, living the family dream in our little house in Kent. Despite my own embattled childhood, I was a good mother and a good wife. Life was rosy.

Except it wasn't. The marriage wasn't great. Peter wasn't abusive or even unpleasant; it wasn't anything obvious like that. It was just that, among all my reasons for marrying Peter, I had overlooked one important thing: I didn't love him, and I don't think he really loved me.

And the everyday stresses of life were mounting. By now we had two very small children, and the economic climate, which had been buoyant for some years, was on the turn. A few months after we'd married, Peter had left his job and started his own electronics business. Then – this was the late 1980s – interest rates soared from a manageable 7 per cent to somewhere around 15 per cent in a relatively short time as Britain swung from Boom to Bust. This meant our mortgage payments rocketed, as did his business loan repayments – our outgoings literally doubled. It was a very bad time to be borrowing money. But luckily, it seemed, we hadn't borrowed that much.

This was an illusion I was to remain under until the sudden death of our relationship. Since I was the one who left first for work every day, before the post came, and because Peter dealt with everything to do with money, I had no idea how bad things were. I never saw a bill or opened an envelope, and Peter didn't confide in me. He told me to leave it to him, and I did. So by the time I realised the true state of things, both financially and emotionally, it was too late to do anything about it: the relationship was over. I came home from work one day and found that Peter had packed and gone.

Shaken and upset, as I simply hadn't thought things were anything like this bad, I took the next day off work. This meant that for once I was at home when the post came. I opened the letters to find more bad news. I was horrified by the size of the mortgage, and that there was no money in our joint account. I was left with absolutely nothing.

The next few days passed in a haze. I remember going to London to see the bank manager – those were the days when people still had them – and, after explaining the position to me (bleak, in a word), he obviously felt so sorry for me that he took me out for some lunch. I trailed home again in despair, taking stock of the situation on the way. I was just twenty-three, with two tiny children dependent on me – Emily three and Alice one – my husband had left me, the house was mortgaged up to the hilt and I had a pile of debts to face.

I wanted to be strong, to be able to cope, but it was all too much. I left my job and went on income support. Soon a letter came from the mortgage company saying they were coming to collect the keys of the house. I knew I had to pull myself together or the three of us were going to be homeless. Clearly I couldn't rent the kind of home I wanted on income support. It simply wasn't practical for me to have a collapse. I had to pick myself up and get on with it.

So, a few short weeks later, I forced myself out into the world again, found a job in London as a legal secretary with a firm of solicitors and rented another little house in a small Kent town nearby. I handed the keys of our house back to the mortgage firm, and we moved. I placed the children with a new childminder, and somehow I was surviving again. The wheels of life were turning once more.

I think it was because I was young that I bounced back quite quickly. Despite the awfulness of Peter leaving and the terrifying feeling of losing everything, once I was back on my feet I looked only forward, not back. But I was never to forget the experience of losing everything, of having to rely on state handouts, and I resolved I would never let that happen to me or my children again. Temporarily, my little family group of three had been so vulnerable – if I hadn't pulled myself together, anything could have happened to Emily and Alice. I never wanted to sail that close to the wind again.

Romantically, my dreams were dented but not shattered. Peter and I might have divorced, but that didn't mean I'd given up on my family dream. It took me a while to get over Peter but my tangled personal life of the past few years wasn't enough to put me off altogether. I still wanted to complete my family circle, and so I continued searching for that elusive Mr Right.

It didn't take long. Once again, the local pub was the venue. I had been working there on the odd evening, and one night Paul, a regular, came in. He was six foot, handsome, with dark hair, and I could feel his knowing blue eyes following me around the bar as I pulled pints and measured out vodka and tonics. I wondered who he was, and halfway through the evening, just when I thought I'd never find out, he came over and introduced himself.

We chatted a little as I worked, and we soon discovered we'd known each other as children — my part of Kent is a small place. By the end of the evening, it seemed a natural step to invite him to a party I was throwing the following week. He told me he'd be there.

The night of the party passed in a blur of faces and jokes and conversation, as they so often do. It was only at about five in the morning, when nearly everyone had gone and I was cleaning up with a few friends, piling up the empty bottles, that I realised that Paul was still there. I'd hardly seen him during the evening and truthfully hadn't given him much more than a passing thought, but there he was, cleaning up with my closest friends. I remember thinking, What's he still doing here, then? I felt a strange sensation unfurling in my stomach as I admitted to myself that I liked this man.

At about nine o'clock that morning, I drove Paul home. He lived with his mother, Jan, and stepfather, Terry. I remember his mother giving me a look as if to say, What are you doing dropping him back at this time of the morning? It was unfriendly, and set the tenor of our relationship. Jan and I were simply never destined to be friends.

Undeterred, Paul and I started to see each other, and, clichéd though it sounds, I quickly fell in love. Attractive, funny and safe, Paul was also wonderful with the children. He seemed a natural father, gentle and loving, instinctively meeting them on their level. He'd always crouch down to talk to them eye to eye, and provoked endless giggles by swinging them in turn up on his broad shoulders. I remember looking up once and seeing Emily perched up there, her little hands holding on to Paul's for security, and thinking, this man is right for all of us, not just for me. Incredibly quickly it was as if Paul had always been there, and the idea of him not being seemed unthinkable. He seemed to offer us all a way out of everything that had gone before, and a way into a loving and secure future. And there is no question that he loved me too. If I craved security, so, in a different way, did Paul. We were a good fit. It didn't take long for us to decide we should be together. This time, I thought, I had all the right ingredients for success.

And yet history repeated itself all over again: as with my parents, there were problems based on our different social backgrounds right from the start.

Paul's family were very down-to-earth, hard-working people. His mother and father split up when he was four and his mother, Jan, subsequently met and married Terry – a successful local businessman. Terry ran a building firm, and Paul worked for him as a foreman. Terry adored Paul and treated him as if he was his son rather than his stepson. It was clear to me from the outset of our relationship that Terry was expecting him to take over the firm in due course. It seemed that my handsome, loving, funny boyfriend had prospects too.

Jan disapproved of me from the start, partly because I wasn't what she had expected for her only son. I think she'd envisaged Paul settling down with a nice young girl who would look up to her. Instead she got me, a woman with baggage in the shape of two small children and ideas of her own. But there was more to it than that. Social differences set us apart.

Jan lived by a simple creed: what she didn't understand she didn't like. Suffice it to say that she didn't understand me. She was wary of me and what she saw as my funny little set of values. Things I rated, like giving my children a good private education above all else, were disapproved of. So we were never going to see eye to eye, but because I was in love with Paul, the clash in values didn't seem significant. The risk of being landed with someone who might turn out to be the mother-in-law from hell wasn't enough to put me off. I knew I'd found a lovely, steady man, a father for my two girls and someone with whom I wanted to have more children. I had found my for ever man, and it wasn't the end of the world that his mother and I saw life quite differently.

Romantically – or naively, whichever way you want to look at it – I thought love was all that mattered. It never occurred to me that if Jan's values clashed so badly with mine, so, given time, might her son's.

Back at the beginning, things progressed quite fast. Paul moved in with me and together we started to look for a house to buy. But even while we were still in the early stages of nest-building, the first sign of our later troubles appeared.

Paul and I had viewed several houses together, but hadn't seen anything that was quite right. Early one evening, when we were due to see a couple of places that sounded promising, Paul simply didn't turn up for the viewings. Assuming he'd been held up at work, I went ahead anyway and found a house that was perfect.

Excited, I rushed home to tell him, collecting Emily and Alice on the way, but when we got home, the house was surprisingly quiet. Paul didn't appear to be in, although his car was in the drive. I went upstairs to look for him, in case he'd been taken ill and gone to bed. I opened the bedroom door and found him asleep on our bed. He had obviously missed our appointment because he'd gone out for a bit of fun with his mates instead.

Perhaps alarm bells should have started to ring, but it didn't seem like a huge deal. I accepted it and got on with further entwining our lives.

Paul quickly agreed with me that the house I'd viewed was perfect, and we bought it. We fixed a moving-in date and gave up our rented house. With a gap of six weeks between leaving one house and moving into the next, we went to stay with Jan and Terry. This wasn't ideal, given the brittle nature of my relationship with Jan, but Terry seemed easy-going and nice enough so I thought we'd manage. But it was while we were living there that I had my first real moment of anxiety about Paul.

I had been feeling queasy for a few days, and my period was late. I was pretty sure I was pregnant, but to be certain I did a pregnancy test at work in my lunch hour. When the blue line confirmed my suspicions, I was thrilled. Paul and I hadn't exactly been trying for a baby, but nor had we been making much effort to prevent one coming along. I felt sure he'd be as happy as I was, and couldn't wait to get home to tell him the news.

On the way home, I stopped as usual to collect Emily and Alice, thinking once again how happy I was that in nine months they'd have a little brother or sister. Once back at Jan and Terry's house, I found Jan on her own in the kitchen. I asked her where Paul was. She told me he'd gone to bed. This struck me as odd, since it was only half past six in the evening. I went upstairs with a slight feeling of trepidation – after all, it hadn't been that long since the last occasion. I opened our bedroom door. There he was, fast asleep again.

Within a day or so I was working hard at squashing down my unease. As I'm sure a million women have done before me, I told myself that no one was perfect, and that if having one too many with friends on the odd occasion was Paul's flaw, was that so awful? The trouble was, I loved him. And we'd gone so far together, it was a shame to back out now. I had two small girls and a third child on the way. I had to think of them. We were moving into the house we'd bought together any day now. Surely it was worth persevering, overcoming this one small thing, and forging a good family life for ourselves?

I talked myself out of worrying that Paul was not the man I wanted him to be, and decided to get on with it.

We moved in. I carried on running the finances – Paul just handed over his wages at the end of each week. He didn't need much money at work – just a few pounds for a breakfast – since he took a packed lunch. Alexander was born, and almost immediately I fell pregnant with Charlotte. Paul didn't seem to mind the babies coming along, and although he wasn't the most demonstrative of dads – no antenatal classes or NCT evenings for him – he seemed to love each one of them as they arrived.

But with a growing family, our little terraced house quickly became too small for us all. Since I'd found a permanent position with a firm of solicitors, which meant I got holiday and sick pay, and Paul had good prospects with Terry, we decided we could afford to move.

Within days we'd found the most wonderful place. It was big enough for us all, with four large bedrooms, a huge kitchen, a dining room and a vast sitting room with stripped wooden floors and an open fireplace. There was a large garden out the back, and a gate at the end of it that led into some woods. It was a perfect family house, everything I'd ever wanted for my kids, in a nice neighbourhood, and near enough to the children's schools. As Paul and I went round it, we kept glancing at each other, our excitement mounting. We knew this was it. We put in an offer, and soon, unbelievably, it was ours.

I began to pack up the old house in the evenings after work. I could hardly believe we were really going to live there. As I pottered about, wrapping up our china in old newspaper, piling books into boxes, I knew the new house was going to be the most perfect backdrop for our family life. For a moment I reflected on how far I had come. Nice husband, three lovely children, a fourth on the way, a fabulous home, a good job. Somehow, I had done it: I had created a really good life, one that was a far cry from my own childhood. My house really did ring with the noise of children playing and squabbling. Their friends came home several times a week. The children knew they were loved, they were hugged and kissed all the time; and although I had my mother's high standards and always kept the house tidy, that didn't mean my kids weren't allowed to have any fun. Someone was always rustling up a batch of fairy cakes, scattering hundreds and thousands across the kitchen before leaving a trail of floury footprints from the kitchen to the playroom. It didn't upset me, far from it. It was how it was meant to be. The fun they had was contagious. I just let things happen, and hoovered up the mess at the end of the day.

Yes, I thought, closing down the lid on another completed box of kitchen stuff, I was very lucky. I sat on a kitchen chair for a second to catch my breath. Physically I wasn't feeling great; I seemed to be suffering from terrible morning sickness for the first time. All my other pregnancies had been a breeze, and I couldn't wait for this one to improve. Still, I shouldn't have long to go. I was nearly three months, and everyone said that morning sickness usually eased at that point. I stood up again, and headed for the next cupboard that needed packing.

Suddenly the old house was all packed up and the removal van booked. I was still feeling dreadful – if anything, worse, not better. Each day I dragged myself into work, but it was getting harder and harder. And then disaster struck with no warning: I was made redundant, effective immediately.

That night I returned home reeling. The redundancy changed everything. The new mortgage payments now looked huge, rather than manageable. I told myself to calm down. I'd always managed to find temporary work before. We'd go ahead with the move – we had no choice – and then I'd look for work again.

We moved in, and my sickness with Charlotte got progressively worse. Soon I felt so ill that I was struggling to keep our three children in order, let alone find temporary work. If I'd still been in my permanent position, I'd have had the security of sick pay. But now we were relying on Paul's wage, and there wasn't enough to go round.

A feeling of helplessness swamped me. I was close to despair. I'd always been a worker, ever since I was sixteen, but now I was physically unable to do anything to bring in the money we needed, and bills were piling up day by day.

One morning, seven months pregnant, with a new stack of bills having just dropped through the letterbox, I knew I couldn't just sit around while the debts that were starting to look extremely threatening piled up higher and higher. I had to do something. I knew it was wrong, because Paul was earning, but I staggered down to the DHSS and claimed some income support. I didn't really know how the system worked, having only claimed once before, but I filled in the form as best I could and pushed it across the counter.

For a few weeks, the little the state gave me helped stretch our family budget further. But my unfamiliarity with the system was to be my downfall. Apparently I had filled out the form wrongly, and within weeks the authorities had caught me.

They told me that they'd prosecute me. I was scared, but hoped for a fine. After all, I had no criminal record, and had committed to repaying the sum I had stolen. I'm glad I didn't know then that a few weeks after Charlotte was born I'd find myself in Holloway Prison for a four-night stay, thanks to a judge who told me that I 'should have known better'. He was right, of course. I should have. What I did was wrong – but I was desperate. But by the time I came out, I had repaid every penny of what I had taken, and was simply longing to be reunited with my newborn baby and three other children.

So the pregnancy with Charlotte, lovely though she is, marked the start of our financial problems. With the prosecution pending and the debts mounting, I knew I just had to get to the end of the pregnancy so I could give birth, get a job and start trying to get on top of our finances again.

Charlotte was born one Friday in May. Ten days later, on the

Monday morning, I was back on the commuter train to London. I had found temporary work as a legal secretary, a six-month contract with a firm of solicitors. The relief at earning money again was overwhelming, and helped offset to some extent the utter misery I felt at leaving my ten-day-old baby with a child-minder. I tapped away at my computer, typing up some letter or other, my breasts bursting with milk that Charlotte was never going to get, knowing my newborn baby was forty miles away from me being looked after by someone else. Juggling the maternal instinct to nurture one's child with the bottom-line requirement of earning a living is something that many women struggle with, but in the early days of Charlotte's life, for me, it was at its most acute. I desperately wanted to be home with her, but simply had no choice.

Also, I was pretty tired. Life was very busy with a full-time job, four small children, a house and a husband to look after. Free time simply didn't happen. If I wasn't at work, I was at the supermarket or in the kitchen, cooking or washing or ironing. But I didn't mind. I had the family I had always wanted, and Paul and I must have been happy in our way, because it was around now that we got married. But no sooner had the confetti hit the ground than I discovered I was pregnant again, this time with Victoria.

By now you will be wondering if I had ever heard of such a thing as contraception. Of course I was crazy, even stupid, to keep having children. They made things worse and worse, in terms of both finances and the emotional pressure on Paul and me. More children simply meant more of almost everything: more lunch boxes to pack, more uniforms to buy, more homework to do, more stories to read, more washing, shopping, ironing, bills. The only things they meant less of were money, sleep and time. But I desperately wanted children, even *needed* to have them after my own terrible childhood, and Paul didn't stop them arriving.

Victoria was soon followed by my last child, Jack. Luckily, through both of these pregnancies I didn't feel ill as I had done with Charlotte, and I was able to carry on working. But although Paul and I were working hard, the financial burden of six children was vast. Slowly, steadily, the debts that had begun to mount when I was made redundant were getting bigger.

In the meantime, the new house, although financially a strain, was proving to be as wonderful a family home as we had hoped. In between my work and caring for my six children, I found a little time to decorate. I hung red voile curtains at the windows of the sitting room, and covered the sofas in red and gold. In winter, a real fire roared in the fireplace. Upstairs, all the children shared bedrooms. Emily and Alice's had yellow and blue curtains, my favourite Monet colours, while Charlotte and Victoria's was a shrine to the Groovy Chicks; Alexander and Jack's had a jungle theme. The rooms were so jolly, and reflected my children's emerging personalities. There was nothing stark or chilly about them, and I didn't even nag them too much about keeping them tidy. I vicariously enjoyed the fun they had in them with each other and their friends.

In a way, our kitchen table summed up my approach to family life. I'd bought it years before, and now I'd found the right home for it. It was really long, capable of seating fourteen, at a push. More often than not, at weekends, on birthdays or special occasions, there were a lot of children and adults crowded round that table, sitting on a variety of chairs fetched from all over the house. On the flimsiest excuse I'd throw a party, and on a day-to-day basis I ran a warm and friendly open house. I always cooked extra in case a friend or two dropped by. It was as I'd always wanted it to be: a fun-filled, happy, open atmosphere where there was always room at the table for one more.

From the start of our relationship, Paul had left the running of the house, finances and family to me. If we had a decision to make, I tried to discuss it with him, but generally he'd say, 'You do what you think is best.' So that's what I did.

As Emily had reached school age, I'd enrolled her in the nearby private primary school. I wanted the best for her. Naturally Alice followed her sister when the time came. It wasn't a cheap option, but I considered it a worthwhile investment – I've always valued a good education, and this small private school seemed to offer that.

The trouble was that, as Emily and Alice had set a precedent, I couldn't not send the other kids too when their turn came. One set of school fees was affordable, two made me gulp; when I took three bills home on the first day of term, I felt like tearing my hair out. Still, I would manage it somehow. Unfortunately the expense did not stop with the fees: there were also school uniforms, the expensive after-school clubs, the music lessons. But the children were so happy and settled that to me it all seemed worth it. We just had to find the money somehow.

Paul wasn't quite as convinced.

In Paul's family quality of education wasn't seen as a passport to a better future. School was just somewhere children went before they got a job. Having been denied a full education, I felt very differently and wanted the best one available for my children. Trying to explain to Paul why I felt it was so important despite the financial struggle revealed to both of us just how different we were. I also realised something else for the first time. It wasn't just his children that Paul was unambitious for; the same thing applied to himself.

For years Paul had been the heir apparent to the building firm, but by now it was dawning on me that his prospects were never going to improve. This wasn't because Paul wasn't capable, but because he didn't want them to. He made it clear that he was happy doing his foreman's job, a job he did extremely well; he simply didn't want to take on the responsibility for the firm. In fact, quite the opposite – he didn't have the confidence or the desire to move up the career ladder at all. I came to realise that opportunity was something that frightened Paul, rather than inspired him, which was a small tragedy, really, as he was good at what he did.

Paul seemed happy with the mundane routine of his life: work, home, have a few drinks, supper, bed. But ambition to improve oneself had been something that I'd grown up with, and it seemed sad to me that my husband didn't share in this approach to life. I found it hard to accept.

Needless to say, as our need for money became increasingly pressing, Paul's refusal to try and build on his career for the sake of the family, if not himself, and earn more money became a serious point of friction between us. Money was now at the root of our growing number of arguments. I was working all hours and bringing in what I could. Why, I demanded, couldn't Paul rise to the challenge and do the same? Why did he allow his lack of confidence and ambition to swamp him, rather than overcoming it for the sake of the children?

Paul wouldn't give me an answer. Instead, the wonderful man I'd fallen in love with had somewhere along the way turned into a silent man who refused to discuss anything more meaningful than what we were having for supper. However I approached him – reasoning, shouting, pleading – the response was now always the same. He would just pour himself a drink or reach for the television remote control. He just shut me out.

So slowly that I hadn't noticed until it was there, a crack had opened up between us.

Life in our marriage was starting to look increasingly bleak. It was as if all the love between Paul and me was gradually evaporating, leaving in its place just a mountain of obligations and responsibilities, and Paul's steadfast refusal, as I saw it, to share any of this burden with me.

It wasn't just the financial worry I longed to share with Paul. It was everything else, too, as it came along; there's always something going on in family life, and I wanted to be able to share everything with him as it arose, in the way that supportive couples do. I wanted him to engage with me about how the kids were doing at school, to tell me how his job was going, or, right now, help me tackle our newest worry, Victoria's health.

Victoria had been diagnosed with a heart murmur at her six-week check, and unfortunately hadn't grown out of it as the doctors had hoped. She followed a special diet and had been doing well, but now she was growing older there were signs that she was having serious hearing problems. She'd had countless burst eardrums, and the GP had just told me that her hearing was down to 40 per cent. We needed to get her to a consultant, but the wait for an appointment was over a year. What should we do about it? Worried, I longed to talk it over with Paul, to share the responsibility for our sick daughter, but he wanted me to deal with everything. 'You just do what you think is best,' he said when I broached the subject, before snatching up the remote control.

I suppose when you feel as alone as I did, that's the kind of time you really need your friends, but I found it hard to admit to anyone quite how out of control my home life was getting, or how bad I was feeling. I was struggling to admit it to myself. After all, my chosen script was supposed to read Happy Ever After. So although a couple of very close friends knew what was going on – Sarah, who lived locally, a sort of surrogate mother figure to me, and Barbara, my oldest girlfriend – I mostly kept it to myself. Oddly, one of the few people I eventually found myself telling the whole story to was practically a stranger. There was a neighbour who often took the same train as me to work each day, and somehow I found myself confiding in him more than anyone else.

David and I had known each other to wave to on an almost daily basis for years: we'd wave across the street at each other as we went into our respective houses, or nod good morning on the station platform as we both waited for the commuter train. Now, in recent months, we had begun to exchange the occasional smile or few words of conversation. Gradually, we began to talk more. It turned out that David worked in High Holborn, five minutes from my office, where I was currently temping for a firm of solicitors. Over our many journeys together, up and down to London, I told him something of my troubles; he was supportive, and I tried to be the same to him in return when he confided that his relationship with his long-term live-in girlfriend was far from easy. It seemed I wasn't the only one in the street who was ploughing through an increasingly difficult personal life.

Meanwhile, our financial situation was ever worsening. With mortgage arrears already an issue, there was no point even considering moving to a smaller house, and the only other saving would have been to move the children out of their schools. But the last thing I wanted to do was unsettle them – I knew just how hard it was to make new friends, knew how moving schools could disrupt a childhood. I wasn't going to repeat the sins of my parents if I could help it.

I recognise that it was my continued stubbornness over this point, as well as my determination to give the children the life I wanted them to have, that was leading us ever deeper into debt. But

I felt so strongly that I couldn't see any way around it. So instead, I did what many people do – I just paid the people who shouted the loudest. The school fees were always paid, so the children could go to school; as was the childminder, an old and trusted friend. We had to eat, so the groceries continued to mount up on my credit card, or if that failed, were paid for by cheque in the hope the bank would be good enough not to bounce it. After that, it was whichever bill seemed the most critical. I hated opening the mail or answering the phone, and I panicked when there was a knock at the door.

Juggling the money that we had was very, very hard to do. The backlog of debts was growing unmanageable, and something always cropped up to ensure the debts got worse not better. Every time I felt I was making some headway financially, an unavoidable new bill would land in my lap.

One of the bills concerned Victoria's worsening hearing problems. I knew by now that she urgently needed to have her hearing assessed by a specialist, but after several calls to the surgery, we were finally offered an appointment over a year away; alternatively, the receptionist told me, I could pay several hundred pounds and see the same consultant the following week. It was a stark choice: pay the mortgage instalment, or arrange for Victoria to go privately to the ear specialist. It took me just a split second to decide on Victoria.

But it wasn't just the children that meant unexpected bills rolled in every month; it was the cost of everyday life. The washing machine broke down and was outside its guarantee; the car needed a service; the house insurance expired; one of the bedroom walls had a bad case of damp. Every month there was something that meant that the backlog of debt kept growing. It was like walking through mud uphill until we had suddenly passed the point where we could ever hope to catch up.

Looking back at everything that was going on – the worry over Victoria, Paul's increasing denial of our troubles, absolutely no money and terrible debts, six kids to look after and a job to hold down – it's a wonder I didn't go completely mad, but I'm not really that type of person. I've always been far too proud for my own good and would have hated to admit defeat.

Of course there were moments when I toyed with the idea of having a screaming breakdown. I remember one time in particular. It was a winter's evening and I was struggling to get home after a long day at work. The train had been late, and overflowing with people; I'd had to stand all the way, with the hot bodies of strangers crammed up against me, on a journey that had taken twice as long as usual. Then, leaving the station, I'd stepped into a large puddle, and my left shoe and foot were soaked through. My shoe squelched as I walked to the car.

It was nearly eight o'clock by the time I got home. As I put my key in the door, I closed my eyes for a second. I'd had a particularly bad night with Victoria the night before – she'd had yet another ear infection – and I was feeling really, really tired. At least Paul will have given the children supper by now, I thought. Perhaps, if I was really lucky, he'd even have given them a bath. Homework would obviously require a miracle.

I opened my eyes and turned the key. As I pushed the door

open, a babble of noise immediately assaulted my ears. I could hear Emily and Alexander arguing over the PlayStation upstairs, and a third child was crying noisily somewhere out of sight. Alice, having heard my key in the lock, was hurtling down the stairs towards me clutching an exercise book.

'Mummy, thank goodness you're home. I can't do my homework, you have to help me,' she said.

'All right, darling,' I said, edging through the crowd of needy children circling me like hungry sharks, and going into the kitchen. The post sat on the table. I could see at least two red bills amongst the letters.

At that moment, Charlotte wandered in. 'Mummy, I'm soooo hungry,' she said, reaching her arms up for a cuddle. I picked her up with a sigh. The kitchen looked like a bomb site. School bags were strewn everywhere, and a trail of games kit lay about the floor. The fridge door stood open, long forgotten by whoever had opened it to extract something – the milk, I presumed, since a glass lay on its side next to a great puddle of milk on the kitchen table.

'Haven't you had any supper?' I asked.

Charlotte shook her head.

Why had Paul not fed the children, not put the school bags away, not got the kids started on their homework? How could he justify this? I wanted to scream. But what good would it do? Instead I closed my eyes and absurdly fantasised for a few brief seconds about a beach holiday, somewhere hot and far away, all on my own. Then I began to count to ten. Slowly.

One, two . . .

It wasn't the kids' fault, I reminded myself. If it was anyone's, it was mine.

Three, four . . .

After all, I was their mother.

Five, six . . .

So I couldn't contemplate walking away from this.

Seven, eight . . .

Besides, it wasn't practical. They needed me, and I loved them desperately.

Nine, ten.

I opened my eyes.

'All right, darlings, let's get some supper on, shall we?' I said brightly, putting Charlotte down and picking up the crier, who had turned out to be Victoria.

'Is your ear hurting, darling? Let's find you some Calpol. Now, what shall we have to eat, guys? How about a lovely cheese omelette? While I do that, could you please put all that games kit in the laundry room, Emily, just leave it there, I'll sort it out later. Alice, sit down at the table, darling, and I'll help you with your homework as soon as the omelette's on.'

With Victoria on my hip, I wiped up the milk, took out some eggs, and closed the fridge, shoving the letters and bills into a kitchen drawer. I found some Calpol and dosed my clingy youngest daughter, before starting to make the omelette and lay the table.

It wasn't until much, much later that I noticed I hadn't even taken my coat off.

*

I tried my hardest to keep life going as normal for the children. Every day I got up, dressed them, packed the lunch boxes, dropped the bigger children at school and the little ones at the childminder, then boarded the train to London. Every night I came home, helped with homework, bathed them, soothed away anxieties, read stories, gave goodnight kisses and hugs, then turned my attention to the house and the preparations for the next day. Paul helped less and less. He seemed to clock off the moment I was home.

Every Saturday I did the supermarket shop, usually with several children in tow. But what had once been simply a mundane event now became a dreaded chore tainted by our level of debt. We needed the food, but too often I found myself wondering whether I would be able to afford to pay.

Juggling the money was a high-wire act. One Saturday, a couple of days before my pay cheque was due, I set off as usual to the supermarket with Jack, Alice and Alexander for company. I knew there was no room left on my Visa card until I made a payment, and I couldn't do that until my salary came through. Nevertheless, we needed to eat, so I'd have to pay by cheque. I had taken the cheque book from the kitchen drawer and just hoped against hope that the supermarket wouldn't ring up for authorisation.

Jack loved the supermarket. He loved sitting in the trolley sticking out his fat baby arms to left and right, pulling everything he could reach off the shelves and adding it to our load willy-nilly. That day I managed to get him to put back the glacé cherries and the bicarbonate of soda, but I knew there would still be a few surprises to weed out at the checkout.

'No,' I said to Alice automatically as she tried to sneak two packets of chocolate cupcakes into the trolley. 'We'll make some at home this afternoon.' I was trying to keep the shopping under the £50 amount my cheque card guaranteed. Besides, I'd always loved baking and didn't have much time for shop-bought cakes full of preservatives. Victoria had a special diet because of her heart murmur, and home-made meant I knew exactly what was in everything.

Eventually we arrived at the checkout with our trolley piled high: fruit, vegetables, a piece of meat for a Sunday roast, fruit juice, milk, cereals, bread, muffins, the usual lunch-box items, loo roll and so on; it was a typical family trolley with no frills. I chose a queue with a checkout lady I knew quite well, and waited for our turn.

My heart was beating a little faster than usual as I loaded the goods on to the conveyor belt, chatting to the checkout lady about her new little granddaughter all the while. I hoped I wasn't going to have the humiliation of having to put everything back.

'Alice, can you please go down to the end and start packing?' I asked with a calmness I didn't really feel. The more food we got packed away the better, I thought, although I couldn't put my finger on why – I was sure that if I couldn't pay they wouldn't let me have any of it.

Finally, it was time. I took out my cheque book and began to write.

'Oh, we can print that,' the checkout lady said easily, taking it from me.

She gave it back to me to sign, glancing briefly at my cheque guarantee card, before tucking it away in the till.

I exhaled. We would eat this weekend, after all.

I know some women struggle with motherhood, finding it relentless and boring. I was lucky. I simply loved it. I also knew I was good at it. I was quite capable of running six children's lives, making sure they had lunch boxes, the right bits of uniform, that they'd cleaned their teeth and done their homework. I had no shortage of hugs to dish out, and didn't mind the relentless domestic angle either: the picking up of dropped toys, clothes, and book bags; the several loads of washing a day; the constant feeding that was required. If our circumstances had been different, I would have loved to stay at home full time; I wasn't working to fulfil a personal ambition. I worked simply because I had to. We needed the money.

My work was incredibly boring, but it paid fairly well and that was what it was all about. Lorna, the controller at the temp agency I worked for, was great. She knew I had loads of kids and was often totally exhausted but was reasonably good at my job, and she gave me easy bookings when she could. By 'easy', I mean doing overflow work in a firm I had been to before where I knew people, and in a location that did not involve too much travelling. This was exactly the type of booking I was currently in. I had been there for about a month and it was simple. The team of lawyers I was working for were very pleasant, overtime was available, which was wonderful, and I could still just about manage to arrive at work on time.

But however hard I worked and however much I earned, the debts were always way ahead of me. I paid a little here and there but it was the tip of the iceberg. The debts had got so big now that I'd almost given up trying to manage them. Lots of arrears letters were shoved in a kitchen drawer, unopened. I constantly robbed Peter to pay Paul, and it was getting to the point where I hardly dared try the cashpoint machine. Some days, we hardly had enough money to get through the day. I cut costs where I could. I always took a sandwich to work to save the lunch money. I mended the holes in my tights with clear nail varnish. I learned how to avoid paying my commuting fare if at all possible, something that went right against all my principles but saved me up to £50 each week. It was a shaming and humbling time, and I knew that it couldn't go on indefinitely. Soon I would have to open that drawer and look what we were facing in the eye.

But still I put it off.

Just when I thought things couldn't get any worse, they did.

It was a Friday. Paul had called me at work earlier in the day and suggested a barbecue, since the summer holidays were about to come to an end and there was no work the next day, so I returned from work that evening to find an idyllic family scene – Paul in the garden, prodding some pieces of chicken on the barbecue, while the kids splashed in the paddling pool.

If only. How amazing it was to think what was really happening once the layers were peeled away. If anyone had looked closer they would have seen two desperately unhappy people fighting their own demons and running further and further away from each other. I splashed the kids, kissing their wet faces and wishing their happiness could last for ever.

Much later that evening, with the children dried off, fed, put in pyjamas and tucked into bed, I was in the kitchen, loading the washing machine, emptying the dishwasher and generally trying to put the house in some kind of order. Paul was asleep on the sofa in the sitting room.

Suddenly, the doorbell rang. I wasn't expecting anyone, and opened it to find two solid-looking men in suits standing in front of me.

'Are you Mrs ——?' one of them asked, after a glance at his clipboard. I was clearly just one poor person on their nightly round of misery.

I said that I was.

This prompted him to go into what was obviously a routine spiel. He told me they'd come on behalf of a debt collection agency and that I should have had several warning letters by now. In my mind's eye I saw the drawer in the kitchen stuffed full of unopened letters. I said nothing and waited for him to go on.

The debt collector told me that if I didn't pay off some of the debt within two weeks, they'd be forced to take away goods to the value of the debt. When he'd finished, I thanked him as if it had been a social call, and shut the door behind them.

I walked slowly back into the kitchen. This time the bailiffs had gone, but I knew that in two weeks' time they wouldn't be so quick to leave empty-handed. I'd have to pay them something, otherwise, as they had made so abundantly clear, they'd be taking things away. I desperately didn't want that to happen. What would the children, the neighbours think if they saw those men walking out with our televisions, our sofa, our armchairs, our stereo systems, even driving off in our car? More importantly, would we lose the house next?

I felt dizzy and sick. I knew that I could hide no longer from the extent of our debt. The time had come – was, in truth, well overdue – to face up to how much money we owed. I went to the drawer in the kitchen where the bills lived, and pulled out the piles of unopened envelopes and the stacks of red bills.

I sat down at the kitchen table, and, with a pen and paper, started to work through them, jotting down the figures as I went along. Looking at the bottom line, I sat in stunned silence, a silence punctuated every now and then by a snore from the living room. I had double-checked my maths and there was absolutely no chance that the figure was wrong. Our debts were worse than I had feared possible. The mortgage was overdue beyond management and we owed thousands and thousands of pounds. What was I going to do?

Chapter Three

On Monday morning I took the early train to London. I had just one thing in my mind: I had to find some extra work to generate more money. After a weekend of frustration at not being able to do anything practical about our financial nightmare, I just wanted to get on with the task of facing up to the problem.

The weekend had seemed endless. I'd spent the whole time feeling really angry inside, while trying desperately to maintain some normality for the children. I felt I was living a double life – taking the kids to the play park, having their friends back for tea, smiling away and being jolly, reassuring Mum as usual, serving up bowls of spaghetti Bolognese, washing hair and reading bedtime stories, while inside I was a quivering mass of rage mingled with fear.

I was partly angry with Paul for not engaging with our problems and thereby helping me solve them, but mostly I was angry with myself for choosing such a bad provider. I had thought Paul would be a good father and an equal partner in the lifelong job of raising kids and all that entails. How wrong I'd been. Now, as a result of my error, the loving and secure environment I hoped would give my children the best start in life was seriously in jeopardy. The penny finally dropped that he could do absolutely nothing to try and dig us out of our financial hell. He was going to continue with his blinkers on, until the rug of our lives was ripped from underneath us. While I couldn't soften the blow that I knew in my heart would one day fall on each of my children – that their parents were falling out of love – surely I could find a way to keep the rest of their happy young lives on course?

Gradually it dawned on me that nobody could help us – there was just one person who stood between my children and disaster. One person who could make sure the bills were paid and the bailiffs turned away empty-handed. One person who could ensure that the lives of my children remained steady, stable, and happy. And that person was me.

I reached this realisation halfway through Saturday afternoon as I stood pushing Victoria and Charlotte on the swings in the local park, and it made my head spin so fast I felt dizzy. £300 a week didn't come close to touching our debts or meeting our monthly bills. I turned the facts over and over, hoping that if I played with them enough they would miraculously change and an answer would present itself. It was like struggling with two pieces of a puzzle that you know have to go together, but which, however you try to join them, turning them this way and that, simply don't fit. Yet they had to fit, they just had to, because if they didn't, my family life would crumble. If I couldn't find the money, we would go under. And I knew what that meant. I had no illusions, after the last time, about how grim and unpleasant the experience would be. I also knew instinctively that if I let myself go down, a drowning mother with six children, I wouldn't be able to surface again. That would be it for us. Last time it hadn't been easy to pick myself up again, and then I'd been twenty-three with two children. Now I was thirty, with six. No, in the pit of my stomach I knew this was it, I had to find a solution, or we'd all sink like stones.

Going under was unthinkable. The upheaval for my children would be immense, disastrous. I knew I couldn't destabilise them like that when they were doing so well, seemed so happy and well-adjusted. I remembered the pain of moving schools, moving house and having a disintegrating family as clearly as if it were yesterday. I just couldn't inflict it on my own children. I would do anything to avoid it.

As on every Monday, the pink-haired girl outside Chancery Lane tube handed me a copy of *Ms London*. Her friend, whose face had more piercings than I would have imagined possible, thrust forward a *Girl About Town*, another free magazine consisting mostly of advertisements for a range of jobs, including lots of secretarial positions that I could do standing on my head.

Once in the office, I put them in my desk drawer. Lawrence, my boss, was not in the office for a couple of days, and I knew that if

I rushed through the morning's work, I could take a longer lunch break than usual to go through the ads. Hopefully there would be something suitable there, some part-time evening typing job, that would pay well and help me dig us all out of our precarious situation.

I shared an office with two other secretaries. Polly was slightly younger than me, and Vera around twenty years older. She had a daughter the same age as me, and came over all motherly, in the nicest way possible. We had become close friends in the year since I had joined the firm, and they had often provided me with a shoulder to cry on when things were looking bleak. They both knew how broke I was, and so were sympathetic when I said I was looking for more work to supplement my salary.

Lunchtime came, and I went through the magazines, circling the advertisements with any promise. I rang a few agencies, emailing over my CV as requested. I crossed my fingers and hoped something would come out of it, all the while wondering how much it would really help, even if something did. After all, how much of an inroad into our mountainous debt was a few extra hours of typing at £10 an hour going to make?

I sat at my desk eating my sandwich rather despondently, pretending to read the articles in the magazines, but in reality my mind was still searching for a solution to my enormous problem, flipping like a Rolodex through the various adverts I'd just read, and repeatedly stopping at just one. It offered a great deal more than £10 an hour, but it certainly wasn't for a secretarial vacancy:

Attractive girls required for escort work. Earn up to £300 per night. Phone——

There was no doubt about it, £300 a night was going to sort me out a lot quicker than £10 an hour. 'Here's the answer to my crisis,' I said jokingly to Polly and Vera, as I pointed to the ad and looked at their faces. Polly laughed, not believing for a second that I was serious, but Vera just looked at me, and I think we both knew at about the same time that I was going to give it a try. After all, I would do anything to keep a roof over my children's heads. And I meant literally anything.

I might have lived a rather straight life, with just a handful of lovers, two of whom I'd married, but I knew that this advert was about sex. About women being paid £300 a night for sex, to be precise. My heart began to thud in disbelief that I was even considering selling my body. But there was no getting round the money – this job was offering the kind of sums I needed. Was this the bloody good fourth option I'd been racking my brains for the other night?

I decided I had nothing to lose by investigating a little. After all, a phone call and possibly even an interview wouldn't commit me to a lifetime of prostitution, or even a night of it, but it would give me an idea of what was involved. Only then, I reasoned to myself, could I make a balanced decision.

I tried to get on with my work, planning to come back and reconsider the issue afresh in a couple of hours' time, but I couldn't shake it from my thoughts. It interrupted my typing, intruded into my letters, and sent my ability to file haywire. The hypnotic factor was the money: £300 per night, earned on a regular basis, would safeguard the life I had now, the life my children lived, and, actually, make it better. Earning that kind of money, I could pay off our debts and afford to do the things for the children that they desperately needed. And I meant needed, not wanted. It wasn't a case of my children lacking the latest Barbie or Spice Girls CD. The things they needed were much more basic and urgent than that. Victoria, for example, needed a new pair of shoes, and at the moment I just couldn't afford them. Her little toes were pressing up against her old scuffed navy blue ones, and I was putting off, week by week, buying her the new ones because we simply couldn't spare the money. Anyone who's got children knows how expensive children's shoes are – the ones she needed would cost me around £40. And that was £40 I just didn't have.

But, went a persistent voice in my head, if I was making £300 a night, I *would* have it. If I was making that kind of money, I'd be down to Start-Rite in a flash, and still have money for the groceries, the childminder, the school fees, the bailiffs, the red bills.

The morals involved didn't really get a look in. I knew, from the second I began to consider the idea, that I couldn't afford to get squeamish about it. I couldn't afford to think, How terrible, I'd rather starve than sleep with someone for money. I didn't really allow myself to think too much about what I'd have to do to get the money I was sitting there fantasising about spending. It wouldn't hurt anyone, it wasn't illegal, and it would get me out of the most terrible financial trouble. How could I not pick up the phone?

So later that afternoon, I went into one of the small side offices when it was empty. I told Polly and Vera what I was about to do, and they came with me, to offer support.

I firmly shut the door on these thoughts, pulled out the advert and dialled the number.

A man answered within a couple of rings. I told him that I was calling about his advertisement, and he identified himself as Jimmy. Jimmy asked if I'd worked before. I knew immediately what he meant. When I said no, he came straight to the point: 'You do know what this involves, don't you, darling?'

'Oh yes, yes, of course I do,' I replied, as casually and confidently as I could, trying to sound like I called a pimp to enquire about prostitution prospects every day of the week.

Jimmy didn't seem to want to talk about the details over the phone. Perhaps he was worried that I was recording the call, that it was a set-up, or that someone was listening in – after all, if being a prostitute isn't illegal, living off the earnings of one is – so I quickly realised that I was going to have to take a chance and invest the time it would take to go to meet him. It might pay off, or it might be a waste of an evening. The only way to find out was by going.

'Can I come and talk about it with you?' I suggested. 'Perhaps this evening?'

Jimmy agreed readily enough. He told me a tube station to go to, and a number to ring when I got there. We agreed on a time, and with the interview set up, we said goodbye.

I replaced the receiver and exhaled.

It was done.

Polly and Vera had been leaning towards the receiver through the entire conversation and had heard every word. Now both of them just looked at me.

'What?' I said. 'What?'

Polly slowly shook her head, a strange look I couldn't quite identify slipping quickly across her face. I think she simply couldn't understand what it was to be in such desperate financial straits that I was prepared to consider selling myself. She was a single girl, whose most pressing financial worry was how to afford a new pair of tight jeans or enough drinks at the latest fashionable club on a Saturday night. What did she know about the pressures of family life?

Vera didn't judge me. She understood. She knew that I wouldn't be thinking this way if I had any other choice. That I was driven by a basic urge to protect my children, no matter what. If Vera had been in my circumstances, I think she knew she might have done the same.

Later on during that long, long afternoon, as I struggled to concentrate on my work, Vera came over to my desk. She made me give her the details of where I was going, and made me promise to ring her when I was on the way home. I protested – I didn't know how late I'd be, I didn't want to wake her – but she insisted.

'Someone needs to know where you are,' she said firmly. I could tell by the set look on her face that no amount of resistance on my part would make her change her mind. I loved her for that – for not judging me, for caring about me despite what I was very probably about to do. I gave her the details, and meekly promised I'd ring when the interview was over.

The afternoon crawled to a close. At the end of the day, I went to the cloakroom. Luckily, I'd worn one of my smartest outfits to work that day – a fitted black dress with a black jacket and my usual simple jewellery: pearl stud earrings, a gold necklace, my gold charm bracelet. I brushed my hair and put on a little make-up – foundation, eye shadow, mascara, a pale lipstick – and surveyed myself in the mirror. The reflection that stared back at me was rather disappointing. I didn't look remotely how I thought a prostitute should look; I looked like a legal secretary. I rummaged through my make-up bag and found a stronger red lipstick. I put some on. Somehow this seemed to me to convey more of the right image. I added blusher and more mascara before staring once again in the mirror. Better. My eyes travelled the length of my body, trying to step outside myself and see how I looked through the eyes of a man paying for sex. Not bad. Except for my shoes. I looked down at my flat, weather-beaten shoes in despair. They were all wrong. I needed heels, not the flat pumps of a schoolgirl. I really couldn't afford them, but nor could I go in the ones I had on. I would have to buy a new pair. Better regard them as an investment against future earnings, I said to myself, and, picking up my bag, set off for the little arcade of thankfully relatively inexpensive clothes and shoe shops around the corner.

Once there, I quickly found what I was looking for in a cheap chain store – a pair of high-heeled black court shoes, stylish enough, and sexy too. I put them on immediately and looked at myself in the shop mirror. Much, much better, I thought, wondering for the hundredth time how it had come to this. Here I was, a middle-class mother of six children, sprucing myself up to fit some preconceived idea I held from God knows where of what a call girl looked like. What the hell was I doing?

Saving your family, that's what, I told myself sternly. I reminded myself that I had no time for morals. Just think of the money, I told myself. This was to become my mantra. Just think of the money. Because that is what it was about.

I got on the tube and travelled to the appointed stop in Hampstead, North London. My stomach lurched incessantly with nerves as I stood in the rocking carriage, clutching my bag, crammed up against all the other hot, tired bodies on the way home from work. As we headed out of central London, the train emptied a little at each stop. Finally, the tube train swung into my destination, rattling to a stop. I got off, and took the escalator to the top. Outside in the fresh air again, I blinked like a mole coming up from its tunnel.

I fished out my mobile and, as instructed, rang the number Jimmy had given me. He answered and instructed me to wait where I was. He was sending a driver to meet me, and he would be there in about fifteen minutes.

It proved to be a long fifteen minutes. I waited at the station entrance, palms sweating, stomach playing circus tricks, new shoes pinching as I shifted from foot to foot, certain that every passerby knew I was on the game. Was the whole world staring at me?

Finally, a black BMW, all smoked-out windows, drew up at the appointed place. I felt like I was in *The Godfather*. Was this really happening to me? It seemed that it was. A very large, well-built man, immaculate in a well-cut dark suit but with a nose that had obviously been broken more than a couple of times, stepped out of the car and walked towards me.

He lifted his shades up on to the top of his head as he drew up in front of me. 'Hello, darlin',' he said. 'I'm Kevin. I'm goin' to take you to meet Jimmy.'

Kevin held the car door open for me and I got in, sending up a little prayer to the patron saint of all prostitutes. Please, God, look after me. I was really trusting to luck here. The door slammed shut behind me. There was no going back now.

Kevin got back behind the wheel and we set off. Probably sensing my nerves despite the casual 'I meet pimps all the time' nonchalance I was desperately attempting to assume, Kevin started to chat, about the British weather no less, and pretty quickly I found myself liking him. I started to relax and talk to him as if we had met in different circumstances. My stomach uncurled a notch, and soon he had my story out of me – the lousy husband, the six kids to look after – and was nodding sympathetically.

It was hard to see much out of the darkened windows, and I've never been sure of exactly where we went, but after about fifteen minutes, Kevin pulled into what looked like a housing estate. As he turned into a cul-de-sac I guessed we were nearly there, and my stomach contracted once more. What would the next hour hold? I had no idea what to expect. I'd never met a pimp before. Would we just chat, or would he want more? Would he want me to take my dress off, to have a look at me? Worse than that, would he want to have sex with me, to 'try me out', so to speak? This ghastly thought was swiftly followed by another. What if Jimmy not only expected sex, but wanted something exotic? To date my sex life had involved only a couple of well-known positions, and I'd never had much more than a flick through *The Joy of Sex*. Suddenly I doubted very much that I had the sexual repertoire required for the job.

My palms really were sweaty now, and my heart was in my throat. What if I was about to make a terrible fool of myself? What if I just couldn't do it? What if I wasn't up to the required standard, whatever that might be? After all, I was a vehicle with a few miles on the clock. Having six kids hadn't left me with the body of a svelte teenager. I was a thirty-year-old mother of six with the stretch marks and gently sagging bust to prove it. And too many suppers eaten late after the kids were in bed had also left their mark, giving me a bit of extra padding in recent years. I wasn't fat, exactly, as I'm quite tall and curvy and can carry a little extra weight quite well, but nevertheless, I was a generous size fourteen. Had I made a colossal error, an appallingly conceited assumption that I was attractive enough for a job like this?

Kevin was walking round to my side of the car now, about to

open my door. Pull yourself together, I told myself furiously. You can do it. No time for doubts, just think of the money. So I thought of the money, and what that money was needed for. I pictured my children's faces, one by one. Emily, with her love of music and the school trip to Paris she was desperate to go on – I'd be able to pay for that if this job came off; Alice, about to sit her exams; Alexander, mad about sport; Charlotte, a sweet little girl about to start in Reception, which meant a whole new school uniform to buy; Victoria, with her squashed-up little toes, and Jack, just a baby.

With their father so ineffective, I was their world. They looked to me for everything, and I wasn't going to let them down. I was going to keep their world stable, secure, the same things happening every day in the way children love. That's why I was here. That's why I needed this money. My resolve strengthened, my flagging confidence returned, and when Kevin opened the car door for me, I stepped out with an upbeat, open smile.

Kevin led the way up a concrete path and into a small red-brick house. He ushered me through the hall and into the lounge. The room was scruffy but clean, with pale walls and two beige plaid sofas arranged around a large television.

In the middle of the room stood Jimmy, waiting to greet me. I'll never forget the first moment I met Jimmy. He looked so much like I had imagined that, despite the rather terrifying circumstances, I had to work quite hard to stifle the urge to laugh. Tall, bald and very tanned – he told me he was just back from a holiday in Los Angeles – he was wearing a white shiny shellsuit and matching white trainers. His suntan emphasised the brilliance of his teeth – his smile was simply dazzling. He was clearly a keen collector of jewellery: he had big gold rings on every finger of both hands, and a huge gold chain hung round his neck, with the medallion at the end nestling against a substantial amount of chest hair revealed by his half-unzipped top.

Taking off his sunglasses, a wide, welcoming smile splitting his face, Jimmy stepped towards me and introduced himself.

'Hello,' he said, 'I'm Jimmy.'

I shook his hand firmly and looked him in the eye, smiling back as confidently as I could manage.

'Hello, Jimmy,' I said. 'Call me Elizabeth.'

I'd given the false name of Elizabeth earlier that day on the telephone, and had decided that I'd stick with it while I got to grips with the reality of this particular job opening. I couldn't explain exactly why I'd hit on the need for a false name, but it just seemed a sensible precaution. I reasoned that there was always time to tell Jimmy my real name in due course, if it seemed relevant. Somehow, I felt sure that I wasn't the first potential escort girl to make an attempt to hide her real identity, and so I doubted it would be held against me if I ever decided to reveal my real name.

Jimmy offered me a cup of coffee, and while Kevin strode off to make it, I took a seat on one of the sofas. Jimmy sat down opposite me.

'Now then,' he said, immediately getting down to business. As he did so, I felt swamped with a feeling that this just couldn't be happening to me. I suddenly felt as if I'd floated out of my body and was looking down on myself from above. It was a bit like watching a play, as if I was just part of the audience. But I wasn't watching. I was here, and it was real.

Jimmy began to tell me about his operation, and how it would work if I decided to go on his books. He told me that he would ring me during the day and give me details of a job for that evening. Details would include the name of the man, where I was to meet him, and when. I would meet the man as arranged, usually at his home or at a hotel. The booking would usually be for two hours and I would be paid £300 in cash. £50 of this was to go to the agency – Jimmy – as a booking fee. The rest was mine. During the two hours, I was to entertain the guy however he pleased, and at the end of the two hours, take my fee and leave.

Jimmy then went on to tell me what to wear: stockings and suspenders, pretty matching underwear; I was to look smart but not tarty

'The client might want to take you out, to a club or a bar, or for dinner, and you need to look suitable for that role,' Jimmy told me, looking me up and down before adding, 'How you look now will do very well, Elizabeth.'

Phew. My agonising in the office loos had clearly paid off. Fleetingly, I felt like a schoolgirl awarded top prize by the head-master.

Having come to the end of his spiel, Jimmy looked at me closely for a moment in silence.

'You're very different from our other girls,' he said at last.

'Am I?' I asked, having absolutely no idea what his other girls were like.

As if to underline the point, a beautiful young girl with long blonde hair and a wide mouth came in at that moment and handed Jimmy a wad of notes. She could have been eighteen; she certainly wasn't more than twenty. I felt like her mother.

'Hello, Jimmy, I just bring my fees,' she said in heavily accented English, an open smile on her perfect face.

I stared at her. I couldn't help it. She didn't look at all how I had imagined a prostitute would, nor did she look unhappy about being one. She looked glowing and energetic and immaculately groomed, with painted fingernails, minimal make-up and eyes framed by well-shaped brows. Perhaps the life wasn't as bad as I'd feared? Certainly the atmosphere between her and Jimmy was very jovial and friendly. This I found reassuring, although of course the whole encounter could have been a set-up. But, somehow, I didn't think it was.

'Oh thanks, darling, I'll take that off the books,' Jimmy said, giving her a goodbye kiss on the cheek.

After she'd gone, Jimmy told me that he had a lot of girls like her on his books; apparently this type of girl was more his norm. She was Russian, he said, as were many of his girls, with about six words of English between them. I gulped. Why would a man want me when he could have a girl like the one who had just dropped in? I wondered if Jimmy was going to turn me down.

'You haven't done this before, have you?' Jimmy asked me, looking at me hard from the other sofa. I'd told him that on the phone that morning, so I was surprised he was asking me again. But maybe he hadn't believed me.

'Well, no, but that's fine, it's no problem,' I said, trying to make it sound like the fact that I hadn't shagged for a living before was merely an oversight, a small gap in my otherwise extensive education.

'You do realise, don't you,' Jimmy asked me, looking me straight in the eye, 'that you have to fuck them?'

'Oh yes, yes of course,' I said, nodding vigorously, wishing I wasn't blushing quite so furiously. My face was suddenly so hot I felt sure I was beetroot in colour. 'No problem,' I continued, desperate to reassure him.

'I mean,' he went on, 'a client might take you out for dinner, or to a play, but afterwards, you know, you're going to have to fuck him, there's no way round it.'

'Of course. Absolutely no problem,' I said again.

Jimmy considered me for a moment longer. He was clearly making up his mind about me. Would I pass? I hadn't even had to take my jacket off, let alone the rest of my clothes. So far, apart from the actual details under discussion, the interview had been as straightforward as the ones I was more familiar with. Those I could sail through standing on my head, but how had I fared in this one?

Finally, Jimmy broke the silence. 'Why do you want this job, Elizabeth?' he asked, frowning at me as if he simply couldn't begin to guess at my reasons.

I thought for a second, and then I told the truth. It was, after all, a powerful and compelling reason to become an escort girl.

'I've got six kids to feed and educate and a mountain of debts to pay,' I told him quietly. 'And there's no one to do it but me.'

Suddenly, with the bald facts of my life hanging in the air between us, I felt more exposed than if I was standing naked in the room in front of him. Jimmy now knew that he effectively held the survival of my family in his hands.

He nodded thoughtfully, and pursed his lips. What was he thinking now? I wondered. Had I misjudged things, had I blown it with my honesty?

'All right,' said Jimmy after a long pause. 'You'll do. Let's see how you get on.'

I exhaled with relief, realising as I did so just how much I wanted – no, *needed* – this job. It represented a way out of all my troubles, and now I'd got it. Jimmy was taking me on. He took down my mobile number and promised he'd always give me plenty of warning before a booking. Then he stood up. Our business was clearly at an end.

As he shook my hand in farewell, he added something which I suspect was for every new girl's benefit. 'Oh, and by the way, Elizabeth, just one more thing: I like booking fees to be paid promptly, you know what I mean?'

'Yes, Jimmy,' I said, 'I know exactly what you mean.'

'Kevin can come and collect it the next day from your office if that makes things easier,' he offered.

In my mind's eye I saw the smoked-out BMW parked outside the firm of solicitors I worked for, Kevin leaning against the bonnet.

'That sounds a good system,' I replied, thinking I could always ask him to meet me round the corner.

'Just so long as it's paid on time,' he reiterated sternly.

I nodded. 'Definitely,' I said. I didn't want any trouble. I knew this was going to be one bill I always paid on time.

Kevin took me back to the tube station, but was quiet on the drive this time, as if lost in thought. We pulled up outside the tube, and once more he came round to open my door. Helping me out of the car, he touched my hand, looked at me, and said something that has stayed with me ever since. Kevin, the ex-boxer, the thug who minded prostitutes, told me he wished that he'd had a mother like me, someone who had loved him in the way that I obviously loved my children.

'Hold your head up, darlin', you're fuckin' special, you are,' Kevin said.

He probably had no idea how his words were to see me through a period of my life that was to be littered with self-doubt and feelings of degradation. I said goodbye to him, and turned towards the tube station to head for home. My stomach still churned – not with nerves, now, but an indefinable mixture of relief and disbelief: relief that I had found a way to earn some cash; disbelief that I was on the brink of becoming a prostitute.

Chapter Four

The call that launched me on my new career came just two days later. I'd been at work for an hour or so when Jimmy rang my mobile and informed me that he had a booking for me for that very evening at 7.30 p.m. Apparently it was with a regular client, a doctor called Mark in his fifties whose wife and children were in the country. He would be delighted, Jimmy assured me, to have my company that evening.

I wrote down the details and put the phone down. Polly and Vera watched me, not saying a word. Well, this was it. If all went according to plan, in twelve hours' time I would have had sex with a stranger. I felt sick with nerves, but not sufficiently to change my mind. I think I was even glad to be getting on with it. After all, what choice did I have? I had gone round and round the rather limited options hundreds of times, and this was always where I came out. This way I'd be able to pay the bailiffs, a couple of red bills, and to buy Victoria some new shoes. I'd mentally spent the money already. Now I had to go and earn it.

Luckily I'd brought some things in from home that morning, just in case. At 5.30 p.m. I went to the ladies' loo and carefully redid my make-up. I had been to Marks and Spencer the previous day in my lunch hour (thankfully that store card was still being accepted) and bought a matching set of black underwear, some stockings and a suspender belt. In the very straight sex life that I had led so far, there had been no call for this kind of kit. I struggled to hook the stockings on to the suspenders before pulling on my new lacy bra and knickers. This new version of me staring back at me from the mirror was rather disconcerting at first glance. I turned away and quickly put my work suit back on before climbing into my high heels. Fully dressed again, I felt faintly ridiculous, and my stomach was leaping about nervily, but the smart and sexy person smiling confidently back at me from the mirror revealed nothing of her inner turmoil.

You, I told my reflection, are about to go and have sex with a man you have never met before. My reflection steadily gazed back at me and smiled, unwavering. She looked cool and collected, which gave my dwindling confidence a small boost in the face of the doubts which were now assaulting me from every angle.

First, I was finally forced to confront the moral issue. I couldn't put it off any longer. I was about to have sex with a stranger for cash. How bad was that? Was I utterly betraying my husband? For some reason, it didn't feel like it. What I was about to do wasn't about love – this kind of sex was different.

And women have sex with people they barely know all the time – as men do, too, I reasoned. And they accept payment, too, one way or another – a nice dinner, a piece of jewellery, a weekend away, free board and lodging. Weren't many sexual relationships actually based on a transaction in some shape or form? Many marriages and relationships were a case of 'I'll look after you if you screw me three times a week'. Even in this day and age, the years of supposed equality, I knew several women who got by in life along those lines. They, like me, had found a way to survive.

In the light of all that, was what I was about to get up to really so bad, something so out of the ordinary? The only difference was that, as a prostitute, the situation was absolutely clear-cut. Love was neither expected nor wanted. With this transaction there was to be no blurring of the lines. I didn't want jewellery or a weekend away. I wanted the cash to secure the stability of my family, and I was prepared to provide sex in order to do so.

No sooner had I rationalised the moral issue to myself than another doubt launched itself at me from centre-left. This was the one I had briefly entertained on my trip to meet Jimmy. Then, I'd been able to shelve it. Now, just hours from a fully fledged sexual encounter, I was forced to confront it more fully. Quite simply, would I be able to do it? I'd never done anything terribly adventurous sexually in my personal life, I'd only had a handful of lovers, all of whom had been pretty conservative, I'd never got up to anything terribly racy. Yet here I was launching myself as a sexual service, so to speak. Would I be able to pull it off, to casually take off my clothes and get on with it in the easy seductive fashion I imagined would be required, or would the guy take one look at my saggy boobs and call it off? Would he ring Jimmy and say, 'I can't believe you've sent me this old boot. Where's my nubile Russian, same as usual?'

And even if I did pass the initial test, what would they want me to do, and where should I draw the line? My mind raced. A shag and a blow job was probably okay, but what if they wanted anal sex? I'd never done that before, and the idea horrified me. I knew from the film *Pretty Woman* – to date the source of almost all my information on prostitution – that I shouldn't kiss on the lips, and that was something that resonated with me. Kissing had always been the most intimate part of sex for me, and the last thing I wanted to start doing with a stranger. While some might think it strange to draw the line there, considering everything else I was prepared to do, to me kissing had always been about love in a way that sex didn't have to be. Kissing, I decided, was definitely out.

Then there was my safety to consider, possibly the most important issue of all. Would I be all right? What if the client was dangerous, or physically repellent, or treated me badly? I comforted myself with the fact that Jimmy had said he was a regular customer. Surely he wouldn't be, if he treated the girls badly? Surely Jimmy wouldn't let him book one of 'his' girls again if he had a record of hurting or terrifying them?

I glanced at my watch. Time to stop prevaricating. Time to go. I smoothed down my skirt and brushed a couple of pieces of fluff off my jacket. My little lacy camisole just peeked out. I knew I looked good with my clothes on, at least. I just had to get on with it. I packed away my make-up, put my extra clothes in a locker in the changing rooms, then, ignoring the panic surging through me, picked up my handbag (containing massage oil and a variety pack of condoms) and set off for the tube and my 'date' with a doctor called Mark.

I got off the tube a couple of stops early and hailed a black cab. I'd planned this strategy earlier as a way of avoiding getting lost. I didn't know the area, and didn't want to have to walk miles in high heels from the tube with every passerby wondering if I was on the game. I gave the cabbie the address and sat back, thoughts racing, trying to collect myself. Stay cool, be calm, I thought. I can do this. Just think of the children.

Within minutes we had pulled up at a large house surrounded by a rather lush-looking front garden, which was shielded by a wall and a pair of electronic gates. I paid the cabbie, and asked him to come back in two hours' time. He gave me a funny kind of look, and said, 'Of course, dear. You take care, okay?'

My face flushed with colour as I realised that I had revealed myself to him. He knew what I was, what I was about to do. It was the way he looked at me, the way he said 'take care'. I could just tell. I pressed my fingernails into the palm of my left hand hard enough to distract me from thinking that this was my life now – forever wondering if people knew I was a prostitute, a girl on the game – and turned to press the intercom bell. The ornate gates swung open, and I walked into the garden and up the gravel drive.

What a place, I thought, marvelling at the ancient splendour of it as I approached the front door. Faded red-brick, it was about three hundred years old, I guessed. These walls had undoubtedly witnessed a lot down the ages. A twentieth-century encounter with an escort girl was unlikely to shock.

Just as I reached the front door, it was thrown open. In front of me stood a rather short and chubby man with a wide, welcoming smile. Despite the circumstances of our meeting, he looked nice. Not sinister, not unpleasant, not perverted – none of the things I had feared. Just, quite simply, nice. A decent sort of bloke. Even as I pondered what the distinguishing features of a pervert would be, a tiny knot in my stomach unravelled. Perhaps this wasn't going to be so bad.

'Hello,' he said, rather happily, as if he did this all the time (which I suppose, as a regular, he probably did). 'I'm Mark.'

'Hello,' I replied, holding out my hand. 'Call me Elizabeth.'

Instead of shaking my outstretched hand – how absurd was I, offering to shake hands with someone I was about to fuck – Mark caught it in both hands and kissed it, then held on to it and led me inside. As I took in the house – wonderful wooden floors, a smell of polish hanging in the air, fresh flowers on the long hall table – he led me into the sitting room, indicated that I should sit down on one of the vast sofas, and offered me a drink.

Although I rarely drink, I was so nervous I accepted this offer without a second thought, on the basis that Dutch courage at this moment was as good as any other kind of courage. Soon I found myself clutching a glass of delicious white wine. I took a couple of large slugs of it as I followed Mark up the carpeted stairs and into the most luxurious bedroom I had ever seen. It was the size of a tennis court, with an ominously large bed at one end. Mark had asked me to take off my shoes at the front door, and now my toes sank into the deepest, softest shagpile.

'I thought we'd start with a bath,' said Mark, leading me through a doorway on the other side of the room to the bathroom. A large marble bath dominated the room. Mark put the plug in and turned on the taps, pouring in a generous slug of bath oil. Then he pressed a button, and the whole thing began to bubble like a cauldron. Oh God, I thought, panic rising in me like wildfire. Paul will know I've been up to something. I'll smell so different.

'Well?' Mark turned to me with a smile. The critical moment had arrived, could not be put off a second longer. I had to undress in front of a perfect stranger.

'Well,' I smiled back, in a manner that I hoped was both seductive and confident. Putting down my half-empty glass, I began to unbutton my suit jacket. I slipped it off and placed it on the back of a nearby chair. Then I unzipped my skirt, and took that off as well. *You are standing in a camisole and suspenders in a strange man's bathroom*, screamed a voice in my head. I ignored it, rolling down my stockings and taking off the belt in what I hoped looked a practised way. Then I sucked in my stomach and pulled the camisole over my head.

By now Mark was down to his boxer shorts, which he was swiftly peeling off without a trace of embarrassment. When he turned to put these on the chair behind him, I saw my chance. I got out of my bra and knickers quicker than Houdini, and slid into the bath. I exhaled with relief at this masterstroke. After all, the water gave my breasts some buoyancy, sending them bobbing to the surface with all the lift of a teenager's. The bubbles, meanwhile, gave me somewhere to hide my lesser points – like my stretch marks. By the time Mark eased his chubby frame into the bath to join me, I was able to smile at him, back in control. First hurdle overcome. So far so good.

Mark lay beside me in the bath, stroking my body gently.

'You're really nervous, aren't you?' he asked, after a few minutes of not-uncomfortable silence.

I nodded, momentarily mute.

'It really is your first time, isn't it?' he went on, smiling at me, his eyes telling me that he was strangely excited by this prospect. So Jimmy had told him.

'Yes,' I said.

Mark beamed at me. 'Don't worry,' he said, with an arrogance I was to see in many clients over the years, 'you're going to have a lovely time.'

He seemed incredibly bucked that I hadn't slept with anyone for money before. It had never occurred to me that the first time one worked as a prostitute could, to some men, be a turn-on akin to taking a girl's virginity.

Mark began to stroke my breasts, my stomach, and my breasts again, while I squirmed inside. I'd come here prepared to touch and stroke and have sex with someone I'd never met before, but I hadn't considered for a second that they'd want to touch *me*. What Mark was doing to me felt awful, so intrusive, somehow much, much worse than me touching him.

Perhaps Mark sensed how much I was struggling. 'Why are you doing this?' he asked. 'You're very different from the usual girl.'

I'd anticipated being asked this question, and I regaled him with a story I had prepared after some thought. 'I have a child, a little boy, and I want to put him through private school,' I lied.

This met with a nod of understanding and even approval, as it would so often in the future. For my wealthy clients – and most of them were wealthy – the provision of a good education was a laudable reason to prostitute oneself in a way that to fund, say, a heroin habit just wasn't. Private education fell within their own sphere of values. It made it all more acceptable, and meant they could, with just a little effort, see themselves as benevolent patrons helping an imagined boy learn to read and write, rather than as what they really were – lonely men paying for sex and a couple of hours of female company.

I'd hit on this story because I didn't want to say I had six children. I was terrified that if I was honest about how many I had, clients would think, good God, this woman's given birth to six children, I won't be able to feel a thing. I'd worked out that that many was definitely not an advantage in this line of work.

Mark's hands followed the line of one of my stretch marks underneath the bubbles. 'Appendix scar?' he asked.

I looked at him in surprise. 'Are you really a doctor?' I joked. 'It's a stretch mark.'

That helped to break the ice. We both laughed, the bath bubbling away around us, as he confessed that his days at medical school were a long time ago. We sat in the bath a little longer, chatting idly, and, despite the strangeness of the situation and what was inevitably to come, I felt myself relaxing a little more. At least he'll be clean, I thought. Mark probably thought the same about me. Perhaps that was why he'd suggested the bath in the first place.

Eventually, Mark stepped out of the bath and wrapped himself in a large white towel. Unlike me, he had no qualms whatsoever about showing his body, although he was chubby and droopy and far from being a pin-up. But I suppose he didn't have to worry about being for sale.

He picked up another huge white bath towel and indicated that I should get out into it. I sucked in my stomach once more, and stepped out. Mark wrapped me up in the towel, rather as I would wrap my children, and used the ends to take a blob of bubbles off my face and pat me dry. It might be a paid-for encounter, I thought, but he was sweet. I suspected he was, in all likelihood, rather a nice husband.

We walked through to the bedroom, and I dragged my mind back to the job in hand. Okay, I thought, this is really it. We've got naked. Now for the sex.

I have an old school friend I see very occasionally, and I remembered her telling me some years before that she had worked as an escort girl in her twenties, and how she always began a job with a massage. This was why I'd come prepared with massage oil.

'Why don't I give you a little massage?' I suggested, in as steady a tone as possible.

Mark smiled in agreement and lay down on his front, one great mass of expectancy. I took out my bottle of oil and tipped some into my hands. I'd never given a massage before, so I was going to have to make it up as I went along.

I began on his shoulders, working them to loosen the muscles, and then ran my hands down his back to the base of his spine, in big circular motions. Up and down my hands went, pressing firmly into the contours of his body, and every time I went a little lower, a little lower, until I was massaging his buttocks too. I was no professional – all I knew was that I had to get Mark aroused. Soon, from his breathing, I could tell it was starting to happen.

My hands kept working while my mind raced. I needed him aroused, but not too far gone too quickly, as I had to spin out the job to fill the two hours. Or was I paid for two hours once he'd come, even if it took less than the allotted time? If that was the case, I didn't want Mark to think I was rushing him, just getting it over with, getting paid and getting out of there. Nor did I want to get him to come so quickly that he had time to rally and demand another round. There were so many things to think about, and all the while my hands went up and down and around his bottom again and again.

Time, I thought, to go lower. As I brought my hands down to his bottom, I trailed them down between his legs, and pushed his legs apart slightly. From his intake of breath I knew I was on the right track, and I started to tease him, taking my hands up either side of his legs, not touching his penis or his balls, but just stroking my fingers up and down the inside of his legs.

Mark was breathing quite rapidly by now, and I felt a flush of success. This really wasn't so hard. Emboldened, I suggested, 'Why don't you turn over, Mark, and I'll see what I can do for you that way?'

He rolled over, a man in ecstasy.

I stroked his chest, his legs, his arms, everything but his penis, which was hard and erect and twitched in an agony of anticipation every time my fingers travelled in its direction. Finally, I trailed my fingers closer and closer to it until at last I enclosed it with my hands.

'Do you like it like this?' I whispered, rubbing gently up and down.

'Yes, but I want to kiss your breasts first,' Mark groaned, pulling himself back from the brink and moving over towards me, pushing me back, and taking one of my breasts in his mouth. He slowly sucked first one nipple, then the other, while once again I struggled with my feelings about being touched by this stranger. However bad it was, I quickly recognised that I couldn't just lie there fighting off feelings of revulsion. I had to seem as if I was enjoying myself. I forced myself to let out a little moan, and to squirm as though what he was doing was making me feel good. Encouraged, Mark began to perform a trail of kisses from my breasts down to my stomach. Then, as if he felt he had done his bit for my pleasure and could now take his without feeling guilty, or perhaps he just couldn't hold on any more, he rolled on to his back again. 'I'd like you to climb on top of me,' he said, utterly matter of fact, passing me a condom and asking me to put it on him.

I took it from him and stared at the little metallic square for a second. I could see the shape of the condom as it lay within its packaging. It suddenly occurred to me that I'd never put a condom on before. I didn't know which way round it went or anything. The irony of this was not lost on me.

No time like the present to start learning. I pulled the condom out of the packet and looked at it before attempting to roll it on to his penis. It soon became apparent that it was inside out. Taking it off again, I took another look while Mark lay back in anticipation. 'Slippery little thing, this one,' I murmured, as I finally rolled it down on to him the right way round. With barely a pause, I threw my leg over Mark, straddling him, slid him into me, and with three thrusts it was all over.

Mark lay there panting for a few minutes, while I slipped off and lay beside him, reflecting that for all my nerves I'd done rather well. He'd certainly seemed to enjoy himself, and while I definitely hadn't enjoyed myself, it hadn't been exactly unpleasant. The worst part had been Mark touching me, when I was not in control; the rest had all been bearable. All in all, I reflected, it had been a success, and not nearly as bad as I'd feared.

Waves of relief washed over me. I'd found a way out of our troubles. I, no femme fatale but a middle-class mother of six kids, could do this, the oldest job in the book. And I felt sure I'd get better. I hadn't done too badly my first time. The next time would be easier, I thought.

A few moments later, Mark and I began to chat idly, as you so often do after sex. At first we talked about the books we had read recently, giving each other recommendations once we had discovered that both of us were passionate about reading. Then Mark brought the conversation back to me.

'I didn't believe Jimmy when he said you were new to this, but you are, aren't you?'

I nodded.

'Are things really so bad, that you have to do this?' he asked.

I nodded again. 'But you aren't that bad!' I joked.

I think he had somehow felt my desperation earlier in the evening. 'If you have to do it, take my advice and be careful,' he said. 'I'm a doctor and I know exactly what you can catch. There are some very unpleasant diseases out there.'

This shocked me. Naively, I hadn't even considered this aspect of prostitution. How stupid of me. Of course there were a range of sexual diseases out there as old as time – Henry the Eighth had died of syphilis, after all, I remembered from history lessons at school – and if I wasn't careful I could catch any or all of them. I listened with rapt attention as Mark now outlined the dos and don'ts of sexual behaviour if a person wanted to stay disease-free.

'Promise me you'll never, ever have sex with a client without a condom, however much he offers to pay you. It's just not worth it. You could get HIV, or herpes, both of which are incurable. And don't let people touch you down there with their fingers unless you've seen them wash their hands. Don't let anyone do oral on you – that can give you lots of nasties too. And if you give a blow job, still make sure the client wears a condom. And however careful you are, you should get yourself checked at a clinic once every three months. Accidents do happen, you know.'

I nodded, speechless, as Mark carried on listing the numerous dangers that faced me in my new line of work. Some of his advice, like never permitting oral sex to be performed on me, I suspected I would have to ignore, but other parts, like always using a condom no matter what, became a key rule in my mentally drawn-up code of conduct for prostitutes. Over my three years, I would be offered vast sums of money to have sex with clients without a condom. Remembering Mark's words, I never agreed, however much they begged and pleaded.

'You're coming to the end of your time. Do you want to go and tidy yourself up?' Mark said.

The two hours were over. I slipped out from under the bedclothes and returned to the bathroom. My clothes were waiting for me where I had placed them a lifetime ago. This time I had crossed the room stark naked. I had obviously more than sufficed. Did it really matter that I carried a little more padding than I should?

By the time I reappeared from the bathroom, fully dressed, Mark had also pulled on some clothes. We went downstairs to the hall and I put on my shoes. Mark offered to call me a taxi, but I told him I had preordered one.

'Right, then,' he said. 'Money.'

He extracted his wallet from a drawer in the hall, and pulled out several fifty-pound notes. I thanked him, and asked if he had anything smaller, as I had to pay the taxi. He peeled off another note, a twenty this time, and gave me that as well, waving away my protests.

'Goodbye, Elizabeth, and good luck with it,' he said, opening the front door.

And then I was out in the garden again, the ornate gates swinging open to reveal my waiting taxi. The world outside was just as I had left it, though so much had happened to me in those two hours.

I climbed in and asked the driver to take me to Victoria Station. I wanted to catch my train home to my family. I sat back, too tired to worry about what the taxi driver thought of me. I was more concerned with what *I* thought of me. What did I feel? Oddly, not much. It hadn't been as bad as I'd thought it would be. I had done much better than I had thought. Surprisingly, it had been quite a lot like a date. We'd had a drink and a chat, a hot bath, sex, a chat and then I'd gone home. Lots of women had dates like that. It was almost as if Mark had wanted it to be like a date, as if that made it more enjoyable, more normal. At no time had he made me feel cheap or dirty. On the contrary, he'd treated me like his equal, as a fellow human being.

Right then I decided that that was how I would always play it – as if I was the girlfriend rather than a prostitute. I was fast realising that I wasn't the typical high-class hooker; I was obviously less beautiful than the more typical eighteen-year-old Russian. But on the upside, I spoke good English, I knew which knife and fork to use, and could discuss film, travel, the merits of private education and, my absolute passion, books, for as long as anyone liked. I was not stupid, and as Mark had showed me tonight, there were nice, decent men out there who were a little bit lonely, who just wanted a bit of company, and some sex. This was a face of prostitution I hadn't expected: men who were prepared to pay for sex, but who wanted the experience to be more than just a romp with a stranger.

My first job was behind me. I found myself marvelling at the 'normality' of the whole event, and reeling with relief that I had managed to pull it off without incident. I could do this job, I knew I could. And as the taxi winged its way towards Victoria Station and my train home, I knew that I would be doing it again. It was a case of when, not if. Because tonight I had found a way out of our financial troubles. Tonight I had earned more money in two hours than I usually earned in the best part of a week. Victoria's shoes could go back on the shopping list.

I suddenly remembered something. I rummaged through my handbag for my mobile phone and dialled Vera's number. She answered on the second ring.

'Vera?' I said. 'It's me. I'm okay. I'm on the way home.'

'Okay, love,' Vera said. 'I'll see you tomorrow, then.'

Dear Vera. 'I won't sleep a wink until I know you are safe,' she had told me firmly. What she would have done if I hadn't rung, I've no idea.

An hour later, I was putting my key in my front door. I was home, and hoped I wasn't about to be caught out. When Jimmy had told me about the job, I'd rung Paul and told him I'd been offered overtime at the office and would be late. Now I didn't want to give him any reason to think that I'd lied to him. On the train, I'd slipped into the loo and taken off my 'working' underwear, and replaced it with my usual bra and pants, but I was still worried that Paul would notice that I smelt different, thanks to Mark's passion for bath oil.

I needn't have worried.

I shut the front door behind me and stood in the hall for a second. The house seemed quiet, apart from the murmur of the television from the lounge.

'Hi, Paul, I'm home,' I called softly, walking through to the living room. No response. My husband was fast asleep on the sofa. I stood looking at him in silence for a moment.

It suddenly seemed as if the day had gone on for ever. My body ached strangely, and I longed to go upstairs, to have a hot bath and crawl under the duvet. But first, all the things I usually did when I got home at six had to be done now, as the clock headed towards midnight. However tired I was, there was no way a child of mine was going to school in an unironed shirt, or with the wrong games kit, or with a less than lovingly prepared lunch box.

It was well after one in the morning when I finally fell into bed, and it seemed like just moments later when the alarm went off at six-thirty: time to get up for a new day. My waking thought was that my new lifestyle was certainly going to be exhausting. But I reminded myself of the bills I would now be able to pay.

On Saturday morning, I set off with Victoria to go to the shopping centre, with Mark's £50 notes tucked in my wallet. Together we chose a sweet little pair of red shoes with rounded toes. I don't know who was more thrilled: Victoria, who insisted on wearing them immediately, or me. As I handed over the money and buckled the shoes on to my daughter's feet, there was no doubt in my mind. None at all. It was all absolutely worth it.

Chapter Five

I had been nervous about going to work the day after my first 'job', uncertain what kind of reaction I would get from Polly and Vera. Would they think I was cheap or dirty, and treat me differently? But when I got there, Vera was calmly supportive, while Polly just wanted all the gossipy details. Phew. The atmosphere in our little office was unchanged. I found this hugely reassuring. It was really important to me that people who knew me before my decision to become an escort girl still considered me a friend now. I needed them to understand, not judge me for it.

Over the next few days, I began to adjust to and accept what I had done. While I knew in my heart that I was the same person I'd been the day before, and that I hadn't done anything that I should be condemned for, I was well aware that society as a whole saw prostitution as morally questionable. Somehow, the fact that it was okay with Polly and Vera, people who knew me quite well, helped. The fact that a couple of people knew what I had done, that it wasn't my secret alone, also helped me get used to the idea that I'd slept with a stranger for money, and was almost certainly going to do so again. And the positive experience with Polly and Vera gave me the confidence to tell another person – someone from my home life – who mattered to me a great deal.

Sarah, nearly twenty years older than me, was – is – the mother I never had. Purely by chance, she also knew Jan and Terry socially, as she was married to Terry's best friend. This didn't stop me feeling confident that her loyalty and love lay with me, and that whatever I told her would go no further.

Sarah had helped me through a lot over the years. She was godmother to Victoria, and was childminder to all my kids while I worked, and even cleaned my house for me when there were simply too many things for me to do. Sarah also knew we were seriously broke, so broke that I was jumping my train fares whenever I could, so broke that Sarah, not by any means wealthy herself, would lend me £20 whenever she could. Sarah was my confidante, she always listened to me and offered good advice, and never judged me. So she knew all about our problems and was therefore well aware that any rescue package was going to have to come from me.

So when I dropped by at her house after work one evening and told her I'd got a bit of evening work that paid over and above the usual rates, she wasn't exactly reeling with surprise when I disclosed the full nature of it.

However, she was furious. She exploded with rage – not at me, but at Paul.

'Bloody boy,' she said. Sarah thought of him as a boy; she'd known him since he was a little kid. She was fond of him, and as her rage subsided it quickly became apparent that as much as she was furious with him, she was also sad and disappointed. How could the little boy with such promise have turned out like this?

'I can't believe he's let it come to this,' she said.

'He doesn't know, Sarah. I told him I was doing overtime in the office.'

'God, you poor girl,' she said, giving me a hug.

'It wasn't that bad,' I protested.

'What can I do to help?' she asked immediately.

At that moment, nothing sprang to mind, other than that she should love and support me despite what I was up to. That was all I was really after.

'Nothing. But thanks, Sarah,' I said.

The task of getting my children back to school for the autumn term took my mind off what I'd done for a few days. Just as important to me as finding the money to pay the school fees was making sure that they were settled in happily.

Emily, my eldest, had thrilled me earlier that year by passing her Eleven Plus exams, and that September she started at the local girls' grammar school. Alice, Alexander and Charlotte were all at an independent coeducational day school which they, and I, loved. It provided a degree of flexibility that accommodated their very

different characters. Alice, for example, was much more interested in fashion than she was at working hard, whereas Alexander
was both a great little rugby player and academically bright.
Charlotte, meanwhile, had to be settled into the Reception class
for her first term.

I was very committed to the school. I had been a member of the
Parent-Teacher Association from when Emily had first started,
and knew most of the mums there. I always played in the mummies' netball matches, was in the mummies' hockey team,
attended all the fund-raisers and never missed the Summer Ball. I
loved that world – it was so far away from all the other things that
were happening in my life – and my children clearly loved it too.

All this strengthened my resolve to keep it safe for them, so that
when Jimmy rang again, I was ready to accept another job.

My second booking, Jimmy told me, was to be in Knightsbridge,
central London, in an apartment near Harrods. It sounded really
promising – it was with a regular client called Larry, I was to arrive
at 7.30 p.m. and stay until 3 a.m., and in return I would be paid
£1000.

Closing my mind to the prospect of what spending so many
hours with a client might mean – what would they ask me to do
during such a long stretch of time? – I focused instead on the excel-
lent wage and what it meant to my family. It would go some way to
meeting several of our more pressing bills. I just had to do it.

There was just one problem. I knew I'd have to tell Paul I was
doing overtime at the office. But until 3 a.m.? What if he rang the
firm to speak to me? Then my cover would be blown, and God

knows what he'd think I was up to – having an affair, probably. I couldn't allow this to happen. I dreaded the effect such a suspicion would have on our already rocky marriage.

I spent the afternoon with half my mind on my typing and the other half on how to resolve this problem, and finally came up with a workable solution of sorts. I decided to tell the evening receptionist that I was going out with some girlfriends, and that my husband would be cross if he knew since it left him at home alone all evening babysitting the kids. I'd told him a little white lie, I said, that I was doing overtime, and would she mind covering for me if he rang? The receptionist gave me an extremely knowing look – I think she thought I was having an affair with someone, which wasn't great for office gossip, but it was better that she should think that than Paul – and agreed that if Paul rang she'd say she wasn't sure whose office I was working in, and that she would find out and give me a message. I gave her my mobile number, so she could call me in the event that Paul rang looking for me.

Reflecting uncomfortably on the lies I was telling, I headed for the cloakroom at work to get changed. I put on my working underwear before slipping my dress back on the top. Soon I was on the tube, rattling my way towards Knightsbridge.

I quickly found the block of flats, and smiled at the porter as confidently as I could as I went into the lobby.

'Just popping up to see Larry,' I said casually, praying he didn't ask me 'Larry who?' Jimmy didn't seem to believe in surnames. But the porter just smiled back and returned to his newspaper.

Larry turned out to be American and in his forties. Short and rather rotund, he was immaculately dressed in a dark suit and a piercingly blue shirt. He greeted me at his apartment door as if I were his girlfriend.

'Hello, darling. You're right on time. Shall we go for a drink and a bite to eat?'

I agreed, of course, and, with him steering me by my elbow, retraced my steps to the lift.

Soon we were sitting in a smart Italian restaurant about five minutes' walk from his flat. The restaurant was dimly lit – to maximise everyone's good looks, I supposed. Despite the relatively early hour, it was already busy. All around me smartly dressed people were shaking expensive linen napkins on to their laps. Across the way sat five or six incredibly slim, beautiful young girls toying with glasses of fizzy water and prodding asparagus spears with their forks. A few of them seemed vaguely familiar – I felt sure I'd seen them photographed in *Tatler* or *Vogue*, striding confidently down catwalks in some impossibly eclectic mix of designerwear.

I dragged my attention back to Larry and discovered that while I'd been taking in the scenery, he had chosen a bottle of white wine. He poured me a glass, and we ordered some delicious-sounding antipasti.

As I sipped at my wine, Larry started to tell me about his work, and how it often took him back to America. I concentrated hard at maintaining an air of interest as Larry regaled me with the working details of the various international stock exchange indexes, nodding and smiling when it seemed appropriate. Larry seemed happy to have an audience.

After quite a bit of this, I suddenly realised that Larry was ordering a second bottle of wine. I looked at the ice bucket – we couldn't possibly have finished the first already; I'd barely had two sips – but there it was, up-ended in the ice bucket, with the waiter standing next to it busy pulling the cork out of the new bottle. I looked at Larry's cheery, ruddy-coloured face and had a sinking feeling that he was just getting started. Oh God, I thought. I could only hope he didn't drink so much that it took hours to make him come. Was that, I wondered, why the booking was so long? I pictured myself jigging up and down on Larry for hours, to no avail.

As it turned out, getting Larry to come was to be the least of my worries. He disposed of a second bottle of white wine in record time before embarking on a third, this time red, to go with his rack of lamb. By now he was in full garrulous flow, telling me in between slugs of wine yet more fascinating facts about his job, and letting slip all sorts of rather indiscreet details about his work companions.

At the end of the third bottle, Larry ordered a double brandy, and I began to seriously worry about how I was to get him home. The flat was only a short walk away, but would Larry be able to stand up, let alone put one foot in front of the other?

Larry was obviously quite a seasoned old drunk, because after he had paid the bill, he managed to stagger relatively elegantly to his feet before lurching in the direction of the door. I smiled, embarrassed and apologetic, at the waiter, who held the door open for us as politely as if Larry was the most impeccably behaved of diners. But something in the way he smiled back at me seemed to indicate that this was not the first time Larry had come to the restaurant and got absolutely plastered.

Once outside, Larry draped his arm around my shoulders as much for support as in a gesture of intimacy, I suspected, and together we staggered towards his apartment block. A walk of five minutes took us about three times that, but finally the lights of his block shone ahead of us.

The night porter saw us coming through the glass doors, and rushed to my aid.

'You all right there, love?' he asked, not batting an eyelid at Larry's state, which seemed to be getting closer to comatose by the second. 'Let me give you a hand.'

With that he heaved Larry's other arm around his neck, and together we lurched into the lift with him. The porter pressed the button for Larry's floor, and soon we were outside his door, Larry hanging between us like a corpse, while I rifled through his pockets to find his keys.

Once inside the flat, the porter turned automatically in the direction of the bedroom in a way which confirmed to me that Larry made a habit of this kind of behaviour.

'There you go,' grunted the porter, as we laid Larry down on the bed.

Then he stood up and turned to me.

'You all right now, madam?' he asked me courteously, as if he had helped me in with an unwieldy hatbox or some heavy shopping bags.

'Fine,' I murmured weakly. 'Thank you so much.'

I wondered whether I should tip him for his help, but before I could decide, he'd turned and gone, shutting the front door behind him.

I sat down on the edge of the bed and looked at Larry, who had now rolled over and was snoring loudly. He had all the appearance of being out for the night. But he hadn't paid me. What was I to do? I'd given up a few hours of my time and cleared my life until 3 a.m. as requested, so it didn't seem reasonable that I should walk away with no money just because Larry had overdone it. I remembered from when he had paid the bill that his wallet was in his jacket pocket, and now I went over and retrieved it. It was bulging with a huge amount of cash – at least £10,000, at a guess. I extracted my agreed fee of £1000, and replaced his wallet in his jacket. Then I picked up my bag, and, taking a last glance at Larry's unconscious form, quietly let myself out of the flat.

Well, I reflected as I went down in the lift, looking at my watch and seeing that it was only just 10 p.m., there must be worse ways to earn a living. I'd eaten a delicious meal in one of the most stylish Italian restaurants in London, helped my drunken dinner partner home and been paid £1000 for my efforts. Feeling rather buoyed, I decided to treat myself. I hailed a taxi, offered him a flat rate if he took me home, and, when he agreed, climbed into the back and promptly fell asleep. My last thought was that Jimmy had been wrong about one thing – I didn't always have to sleep with them, after all.

*

My next job was the first to take me outside London. The client, a man called Simon, lived in Berkshire – hardly the most convenient place for me, but I didn't dare to turn it down in case Jimmy took it as lack of interest and didn't ring me with any more jobs. So I accepted immediately and decided to worry later about how I was going to get there. Sometimes Kevin would drive me to jobs apparently, but that wasn't possible with this one. I had to get there under my own steam.

I wrote down the details and thanked Jimmy before hanging up. Sitting back in my chair, I thought for a moment. How on earth *was* I going to get there? Trains weren't going to work – I'd never get home afterwards. Since I had a bit of notice (the job wasn't until the following evening) I decided that the best thing to do was to drive myself.

So the next day, after work, I found myself dressed once again in what I was coming to think of as my working kit. Matching bra and panties, stockings and suspenders, and a dark dress on top. I had on my usual amount of jewellery – earrings, a necklace, my charm bracelet – and the obligatory high heels.

After asking for directions at a local petrol station, I found the road without too many problems. I drove slowly along, looking for the right number. Parking the car outside the house, I locked up and walked determinedly up the front path. Here we go again, I thought as I rang the bell. I was still a little nervous, but not nearly as much as the very first time.

The man who opened the door was obviously extremely fit. He was wearing a short-sleeved T-shirt and a pair of tight jeans, revealing a very well-worked-out body. With short dark hair, he struck me as a rather good-looking man. Why on earth, I wondered, did a man like him need a hooker? Surely the girls were queueing down the street.

He smiled at me. Nice even white teeth. 'Hello, I'm Simon,' he said.

'Hello,' I smiled back. 'I'm Elizabeth.'

Simon offered me a drink, and I soon found myself clutching a glass of white wine. I took a few huge sips as Simon studied me for a moment. Then I followed him upstairs, and, drawing on my burgeoning experience, suggested in what I hoped was a seductive way that perhaps we should have a bath together. I'd cottoned on that this was a good way to start, on the basis that, this way, whoever I had been paid to have sex with would, at least, be clean.

Simon agreed willingly and we went through to his bathroom. Less luxurious than Mark's, as 99.9 per cent of bathrooms surely must be, it was nevertheless clean and bright, with a large bath in one corner. I put in the plug, turned on the taps, and asked Simon not to put in any bubbles, telling him my skin was rather sensitive. In reality, I didn't want to give Paul any cause to suspect that I was up to anything. So far I had got away with it, but I still had to be cautious, just in case. I knew Paul's disapproval of what I was up to would be extreme.

I eased out of my clothes, rolling down my stockings in the casual way girls did in old movies, and feeling rather pleased about that. I was learning.

When I turned, naked, and stepped towards the bath, Simon

was in front of me, starkers, with a huge erection. This kind of evidence of my success gave me a boost. It made it clear that the battle, if it was one, was already won. Tonight Simon clearly liked what he saw.

'Down, boy!' I giggled, and, taking his hand, led him towards the bath.

In the bath, we sat at opposite ends, talking about nothing in particular to get things going. I asked him what he did, and he said he was in security. That explained the body, I thought. He asked me about myself, and I told him my cooked-up story, that I was working to educate my son. All the while, as we chatted, I stroked his toes and his ankles, and massaged his feet a little, my hands made slippery with a bar of soap. As the conversation paused, I began to work my way up his legs, inching up a little more each time, until I was kneeling up in the bath and leaning towards him, breasts swinging, my gold necklace dangling between them. I could tell he was mesmerised by them, and could feel his longing to touch them. Emboldened as my hands went higher, I stroked his balls and his prick under the water. I didn't linger long, as I suspected if I did it would all be over too quickly. Instead I playfully splashed water at his chest and suggested we get out and go and lie down.

He agreed as meekly as a little lamb. We dried off and went next door, and Simon lay down on the bed. I took out my bottle of massage oil, and began to oil him up. I felt much more in control than I had with Mark. My confidence was already growing, even though this was only job number three – well, two.

Simon was writhing under my hands as I stroked his back down to his bottom, and then slowly down between his legs, perfecting the routine I had begun at Mark's.

'Why don't you roll over?' I said, and he did.

Soon, after a little more stroking, it was clear that Simon couldn't hold on much longer. Every time my hands went near his prick, he was gasping like a man about to come.

'Shall I fuck you?' I whispered. 'Would you like that?'

He nodded in ecstasy, unable to speak.

I extracted a condom from my bag and this time got it on first time. I climbed on top of him and eased myself down. Simon gurgled like a drowning man as I moved up and down on him, sliding his cock in and out of me. Then, with a few gasps, his head went back, and he was coming.

I waited a minute or so for him to recover, and then climbed off and lay beside him. I'd done it. Mission accomplished. Would all my clients be this easy?

'God, that was good,' Simon said, rallying, raising himself up on one elbow and looking at me. 'Jimmy said you were new to this, but you seem very good at your job to me.'

I took this as a compliment. 'I am new to it,' I admitted. 'I've only been doing it for a few weeks.'

After a few moments, Simon said slowly, 'It's not the sex that gives you away as a novice. The sex is great. It's the way you act.'

'What do you mean?' I asked, puzzled.

'You're just asking to get yourself murdered,' he replied.

I felt a frisson of fear crawl up my spine. Simon seemed so normal. Had I just screwed a maniac? Would he strangle me with my own stockings? Suddenly I could see the headline: NAKED ESCORT GIRL FOUND MURDERED IN DITCH.

'I'm in security, so I should know,' he went on. 'You've left yourself vulnerable several times this evening. In security terms, you're just making so many mistakes. If I was a maniac – don't look so worried, I'm not – it would be very easy to kill you.'

I exhaled. Perhaps I was going to live to see another day after all. 'What do you mean?' I asked.

'Well, first off, you accepted a drink. How do you know I didn't spike it? I could have put anything in there, had you unconscious in five minutes.'

I looked at him. 'Did you?' I asked, alarmed. I certainly felt normal enough.

'No,' said Simon. 'Like I said, I'm not a maniac, I'm just a guy who wants a shag. But not all of your clients will be like me. You've got to dump the naivety, pronto. This is a risky business you've gone into, Elizabeth, and a nice girl like you, a lady with a child to think of, you've got to be prepared in the event you meet someone nasty.'

What Simon was saying was waking me up to the risk of my new career. I had to wise up, learn to look after myself – and fast. After all, the very next client I went to could be the weirdo. Unlikely, but possible, and I had to be prepared for that.

'What else am I doing wrong?' I asked.

'Take a look at your jewellery. Hoop earrings, easy for a man to rip off in a struggle. Your necklace is one long thick chain, a person couldn't ask for anything more perfect to strangle you with.'

I paled, but Simon went on. 'And it's got a cross on it – what if the guy hates Christians? Never wear anything that personalises you, that gives away your preferences, reveals anything about who you really are. It might wind someone up the wrong way, enough to tip them over into getting violent. And then there's your shoes. Incredibly high heels, I noticed. Very sexy, but not great for running in, are they?'

I shook my head, dazed. None of this had occurred to me.

'Always wear something with a heel low enough for you to run in if you have to. And preferably with an ankle strap, to hold it on.'

'Okay,' I muttered, suddenly realising, after my flush of success over the sex, that I wasn't so clever after all.

But Simon wasn't finished. 'Did you watch me lock the door?' he demanded.

I shook my head again. It simply hadn't occurred to me.

'Well, how are you going to know how to get out in a hurry, then? Always watch the door close, whether they lock it, and if they do, how you'd unlock it in a hurry if you had to. If they lock it and take the key out, you know the job's bad news and you should think of a reason to get out of there, fast.'

My heart was thudding in my chest by now. Of course I'd considered that I ran the risk of meeting a weirdo in this job, but it was only now that Simon was hammering out the dangers that faced me, one by one, that I truly felt afraid.

He must have read something of this on my face. 'Look,

Elizabeth, hopefully you won't need any of this advice and nothing horrible will ever happen to you. But just in case, take precautions. Be careful. That's all I'm saying. You'd do well to remember all this.'

I nodded vigorously. Of course I would. I had made a serious mental note. Several. From now on it would be stud earrings only, no necklace and shoes with ankle straps. I'd pay attention to the door on the way in, and wouldn't accept any more drinks.

'Is there anything else I should know?' I asked.

'Yes, actually, there is. Did you drive here tonight?'

I nodded.

'Well, leave your car unlocked and keep a spare set of car keys in the side pocket of the driver's door, just in case you have to make a run for it. Keep your handbag with you at all times, and don't keep anything in it that might identify you. That means no bills, no personal letters, no diary – no personal details. You don't want a client to rummage through it and find, say, a bill that gives him your real address. Or name, come to that,' Simon added with a knowing smile. 'I presume you've got enough sense to be called something other than Elizabeth in your real life?'

I gaped at him, momentarily speechless. 'What were you in the SAS, James Bond or something?' I asked.

'Ah, I could tell you, but I'd have to kill you afterwards,' Simon grinned. 'Official Secrets Act, you know.'

I smiled back, reflecting how fortunate I was that amongst my first bookings as a working girl I had encountered a doctor who had advised me on how to keep the health risks facing me to a minimum, and a security expert who had briefed me fully on safety. I fleetingly wondered if this was all part of Jimmy's induction package, or just coincidence. Whatever the answer was, I knew I was fortunate. I had already taken Mark's words of warning very seriously indeed, and now I was going to follow Simon's advice to the letter. Between the pair of them they could write a handbook: *An idiot's guide to prostitution* . . .

It was time to get dressed and go. Back downstairs Simon extracted a handful of notes from his wallet. I took them without any embarrassment this time. I'd done a job and was merely being paid for it. I tucked them away in my handbag, thanked Simon, and left.

As I walked back to the car, it struck me forcefully that it wasn't the sexual intimacy with a stranger that was the oddest part about being a working girl. It was the mental and emotional relationship that was built up in a short space of time, secure in the knowledge that you'd very probably never see that person again, unless they decided to invite you for a repeat booking. I wondered what I knew about Simon after our two-hour encounter that some of his long-term friends quite possibly didn't.

I also felt amazed at how proactive and enthusiastic about life some men could be. I suppose I'd got used to Paul, the lump on the sofa, refusing to help me with anything, simply pretending I wasn't there. In contrast to him, these clients seemed full of energy for life, busy with their jobs and aspirations. Nor had I expected the level of interest in me as a person they expressed. It was a surprise to me that someone like Simon cared sufficiently about a fellow human being not to condemn me for being a working girl, but instead to give me what advice he could to keep me safe and well in the job.

Being a working girl was turning out quite differently from how I had imagined.

After that, Jimmy began to ring me about twice a week. Each time I would call Paul and tell him I'd been offered some overtime at work, so would be home late. He accepted it as easily as a bird swallowing a worm. He simply didn't care enough to be suspicious. So long as no one bothered him and he could have a drink in front of the TV, he was happy.

The jobs continued to turn up surprises, but not unpleasant ones. I came to realise that most clients were simply rather lonely men looking for a bit of company and some fairly straightforward sex. Up to now I hadn't been asked for anything more adventurous than a blow job. My horror of being asked for anal sex or some such had so far come to nothing.

Nor did Larry turn out to be the only client who paid me for sex only to fail to have it. Most of the time sex occurred, but occasionally a man just wanted to chat to an 'attractive woman', to have someone to share the details of his life with. There are a lot of lonely people in the world . . .

Increasingly, I wondered if this was all I should come to expect from clients. Were most of them going to turn out to be quite normal types, with interesting jobs and lives, just sexually frustrated and probably a little lonely? Certainly so far they were a far cry from the sleazeballs I had imagined it entirely possible that I might encounter in this game. Each job seemed a little easier than the last. The men might not be much to look at, but my bath routine meant they were clean. And all of them had treated me well.

But while the jobs weren't as bad as I'd initially feared, I found myself worrying about the children. Had they eaten properly? Had they gone to bed at the right time? Had Paul made sure they'd done their homework? Would he remember to put the washing on, or make sure the kids' PE kits were ready for the morning?

While I worried about leaving everything to Paul, I also knew that I had no choice but to go to work for the sake of us all. I'd been round that circle countless times without finding an alternative, and now that I'd made the emotional adjustment to the fact that I was an escort girl, I was beginning to enjoy watching the money I was now earning making rather dramatic inroads into our debts.

I was being paid around £300 for every job, as well as getting generous tips of anything up to £50. By doing a couple of jobs a week on top of my legal secretarial work, I was taking home over £1000 a week. It had given me enormous satisfaction to be able to answer the door to the bailiffs with a smile on my face when they made their promised return visit and hand them an envelope of cash. The surprised look on their faces told me that not many people in as much debt as we were managed to achieve this. But I'd pulled it off, and now I was using the rest of the money to pay the most pressing of our red bills and arrears.

Admittedly I was even more exhausted than usual, but knowing I was doing something to safeguard my family gave me the energy to continue. However, I knew I couldn't keep going at such a pace indefinitely. I was accepting every booking Jimmy gave me, but what if he offered me more? Three nights a week, four, or even five? How would I manage daytime work as well?

A small thought had taken root in the back of my mind at about this time, and now it kept working its way to the fore. One night as a working girl brought in the same amount of money as one week as a legal secretary. Because of my full-time day job, I simply couldn't manage more than a couple of evening bookings a week if I was also to run the home and look after the kids properly. Even as things stood, all food shopping and other major household chores were now relegated to the weekends.

But what if I gave up my day job?

At first I kept pushing this thought away. It was a momentous step, after all. To derive one's full income from prostitution seemed much more of a significant step than just taking on the occasional evening booking. But my mind kept doing the maths and coming up with sums like £2000 a week take-home pay. By working five or six nights a week I would, at the very least, double what I was taking home now. I might very well earn more than double. I allowed myself to imagine the impact this kind of money would have on our debts. I imagined the kitchen drawer no longer bulging with red bills; I saw the letters from the mortgage company no longer dropping on to the door mat with such threatening regularity. I pictured Emily's face when I told her she could go on the school choir trip to Europe, as she longed to do.

All this would be possible if I took the plunge and became a

126

full-time escort girl. I mulled the idea around a bit more. If I gave up my day job, I'd be around for the kids in the day, I'd be able to go to their special assemblies and ballet performances. I'd be able to pick them up from school and the childminder each day, and I'd get on top of the household tasks. And, if I made sure I never took a job before about 8 p.m., I'd be able to settle the little ones every night before I went out, and feed and bath the older ones and get their homework done. I hated missing out on all these things. The thought of being much more involved in their daily lives was tempting. How ironic that by becoming a full-time escort girl I would see much more of my kids.

But would there be enough work for five nights a week? How could I be sure? Recognising that this, rather than my personal feelings, lay at the crux of this decision, I resolved to do a little research into the matter. And that meant going back to *Ms London* and the free ads.

I remembered that, when Jimmy's ad had first caught my eye, there had been a number of others advertising similar services. Digging out an old copy from the bottom drawer in my desk, I turned to the back and circled a couple that sounded promising. In my lunch hour, I nipped into a quiet side office and started to work through the numbers.

The first couple of agencies were based in North London and told me they could give me a few nights' work a week. I wasn't sure this would be enough. The third call proved more fruitful. This was to an agency in South London that apparently required escort girls for regular work.

A woman called Holly answered the phone. I expressed my interest in her advertisement, and was able to answer her question of whether I had worked before with a confident affirmative.

'Yes, I've worked part-time for the last few months,' I told her, exaggerating my experience a little. In truth it had been a matter of a few weeks since I had placed a similar call to Jimmy.

This went down well. 'That's good, darling.'

Holly began to outline how the agency worked. She told me that the agency fee was £30 per booking (great, I thought) and that an hourly booking was charged at £150. Obviously if I visited a couple I would be paid more. I tried not to splutter in shock down the telephone at this, as up until now, the idea of visiting a couple for a threesome simply hadn't occurred to me. A blow job was the most exotic I had got, to date.

'Okay,' I croaked, before Holly continued.

The safety of her girls was paramount, Holly said. Each girl had a driver, who took her to each job and waited outside until she had finished. Then he took her on to the next one, or, if it was the end of the night, home. He was paid, by the escort girl, £25 per booking. Despite the extra cost, I liked the sound of this. And actually it only brought the total charge on my earnings up to a little above what I was paying Jimmy per job anyway, with no consideration for my safety at all.

Holly outlined her policy on safety a little further: she told me that every client who called in had to give a landline number – a mobile wasn't considered enough. Before the booking was confirmed, the agency rang the client back on the number given to check it was a genuine booking. All this sounded good to me.

'And how much work do you think you could get for me?' I asked.

'Several bookings a night if you want it, darling,' she replied crisply. 'On average you would take home about £400 each evening, if you did a couple of bookings a night. Of course if you took more bookings, you could make considerably more money. But that's up to you to decide. All I can say is that I can certainly guarantee you work five or six nights a week, as you choose.'

'Guarantee?' I queried. Was she really that sure of the demand?

'Oh yes, darling, no problem. We're awash with clients, just awash, and good girls are hard to find.'

I thanked her for her time, and asked if I could make an appointment to see her. That would give me the time I needed to decide whether I was really ready for this – ready to become a full-time escort girl.

'Oh, you don't need to meet me, darling,' Holly said. 'Just give me a ring when you've decided, and we can get started straight away.'

I replaced the receiver and looked down at the desk. On the pad in front of me I noticed I'd scrawled '£400 per night' and ringed it several times. That was the sum I could take home. If I worked six nights a week, I would soon be making really serious inroads into our debts. Most importantly, I'd be able to afford to start making regular big payments to catch up with the mortgage, and then we'd definitely be able to keep the house.

This was a big issue facing me just then. A few days previously, I'd received a summons to attend a repossession hearing. The building society had had enough of my excuses. Now they wanted the house back. Of course I couldn't bear the thought of losing our home. I loved it, my kids loved it, and the idea of giving it up filled me with dread. From my time as a legal secretary, I also knew how repossessions worked. I knew that if the building society had their way, they'd put it on the market at a price that would cover the mortgage but not our equity. At such a low price, it would sell in a flash. This would ensure that the building society was repaid in full; but we would see nothing of the equity we'd originally put into it. Everything we'd ever had would be lost.

I sighed. Since my decision was driven entirely by our circumstances – the money I earned would save our family home and ensure that the stability of my children's lives continued – I knew in my heart that I'd already decided. I didn't feel excited about it, or pleased. To be frank, I felt rather exhausted at the mere thought of having to sleep with so many men. But I knew that I'd have to work as an escort girl for a much shorter length of time if I resigned my job with the solicitors and went to work for Holly full time than if I stayed with Jimmy part-time and carried on my secretarial work too.

I also knew that lying to Paul, and other people, something that was already starting to get to me, would be made easier if I could simply say I had one full-time night job. At the moment, I often had to cobble together fairly unbelievable stories and rope in third parties to my deceit, as I had with Larry. It felt like I was creating a fragile network of lies that could all too easily be revealed. I worried constantly that Paul would suddenly twig that my secretarial overtime hadn't operated like that in the past, and would get suspicious.

But if I went to work for Holly, I could say I'd been offered a full-time word-processing night job. Then Paul would expect me to be out most of the night, five or six nights a week. I knew enough about that kind of secretarial work to be convincing. With a more believable alibi, I'd be free to entertain what Holly assured me would be a good, steady flow of clients that might keep me up until 3 a.m. most nights, no questions asked. There was also the advantage that a night job doing secretarial work paid more than my day job, and that would help me answer any queries Paul had about how I was managing to bring down our debts. In the event that he asked, of course. To date he hadn't shown any interest whatsoever in why the bailiffs had gone away or the building society had stopped hounding us, I reflected, just a little sourly.

No point thinking like that, I told myself, pushing the negative emotions away. It simply didn't help. I ripped out the page with '£400 per night' scrawled on it, screwed it up and chucked it into the bin. £400 per night was our salvation, but was I selling my soul to get it?

I walked slowly back to my own desk and sat down. After a minute, I turned on my computer and began to type out my letter of resignation.

Chapter Six

Switching from full-time secretary to full-time call girl was a surprisingly swift and easy transition. Making the decision had been the hard part; putting it into practice was almost ludicrously simple.

The law firm accepted my resignation without question, largely because my boss was well-known throughout the firm as a short man with a large temper; most people were amazed that I'd lasted the year or so that I had. Only a few days previously he'd had a full-sized tantrum, sweeping phones on to the floor and throwing files about while shouting at anyone in his way, so I didn't need to invent a reason for my departure. All the same, some people – Vera, Polly and a few other work colleagues – were sad to see me go.

As for me, although part of me felt sad, I couldn't afford to look back. Money was driving me, and I simply couldn't allow my personal feelings to swamp me. Of course I didn't want to have sex with strangers every night of my life, but I knew I had no choice.

So, maintaining my tunnel vision, and refusing to allow myself to think too hard about what being a full-time escort would mean, I simply focused on the benefits to the family and got on with the practicalities.

Joining Holly's agency was easy. When I rang back just hours after my first call, Holly remembered me from our earlier conversation and agreed to sign me up straight away. I gave her my mobile number, and told her I definitely wanted to work six nights a week, with several jobs a night if possible. I also gave her a start date coinciding with my last day at the law firm.

Holly introduced me over the phone to the other girl operating the phones – a motherly-sounding woman called Trish. More often than not, apparently, it was Trish who ran the switchboard, taking calls from clients and allocating them to the girls. I realised immediately that she was someone it was important to make a good impression on if I wanted a steady stream of jobs. As it turned out, I was one of the most reliable girls the agency had from the day I joined, and Trish and I hit it off from the start.

After that call was over, I thought for a moment, then picked up the phone again. This time, I was calling Jimmy. I told him a little white lie – that I just couldn't do it any more. I didn't want to tell him I was going elsewhere – it didn't seem very polite or kind. He'd given me my first opportunity, after all.

'Fair enough, love,' was all he said. 'I never expected you to last very long in this game.'

Little did he know, I thought, replacing the receiver slowly. Little did he know.

With those essential calls out of the way, I turned my mind to the next task in hand: equipping myself suitably for the demands of my new career. A couple of the clients I'd visited while I was with Jimmy had asked me if I had a vibrator. Then, new to the game, I hadn't. Not wanting to reveal this, I had told them I had, but that it was broken. Now things were different. If I was going to work seriously as a call girl, a little bag of tricks containing some suitable toys was something I ought to build up.

At home that evening, when the kids were in bed and Paul was downstairs in front of the television, I looked out a small, smart overnight case from our storage cupboard. Into it I packed my sets of working underwear – I had three by now, in red, white and black, all from dependable Marks & Spencer; they washed so well – as well as a bag of toiletries which included some massage oil and some condoms in a variety of textures and colours.

I looked down at the case. It was about a quarter full: plenty of room for the extra stuff I needed to acquire. But even without the variety of vibrators it would contain once I'd been shopping, I knew it would be a disaster if Paul found it. Getting round him had been straightforward enough – just as I'd anticipated, when I told him that I had been offered a full-time night word-processing job that paid much better than my current secretarial work, he had accepted the change without question – but if he came across this, difficult questions would be asked.

I had to keep it somewhere out of Paul's reach. I cast around for ideas, quickly discounting the obvious: the back of the cupboard, the boot of the car. Too risky. Suddenly Sarah's voice floated into my head. 'If there's anything I can do to help . . .' I made a quick decision. I carried the case quietly downstairs and out to the car, then I nipped back to the sitting room.

'Just popping over to Sarah's for half an hour,' I told Paul, who was sitting on the sofa, feet up on the coffee table, watching football. His eyes didn't even leave the television as he grunted his reply.

I hopped into the car and drove to Sarah's house – she only lived five minutes away. I hoped she wouldn't mind what I was about to ask her to do.

I rang the bell and waited, suitcase in hand.

'Hi, Sarah,' I said, as she opened the front door.

'Hello, love, come in. Everything all right?' she asked, her eyes taking in the suitcase.

'Yes, fine, but I need to ask you a favour. Somewhere private, if you don't mind,' I added, unsure if her husband, Bill, was at home. Bill was lovely, but I didn't feel I necessarily had to burden him with the details of my new working life.

'It's okay, Bill's out,' Sarah said.

'Oh. Okay. The thing is, Sarah, I've decided to give up my secretarial job and work nights full time. And I need somewhere to hide my little overnight bag. Where I can be sure Paul or the kids won't find it.'

Sarah took this in her stride. She didn't so much as blink.

'Of course, love, no problem. How about the garage? That way you can collect it or drop it off even if I'm not here,' she said.

'Thanks, Sarah, you're a real friend.'

And so, as easily as that, I had set up a system that would work brilliantly for the next three years.

A couple of days later, the end of my employment at the solicitors fast approaching, I set off on a shopping trip with a difference. I slipped out of the office early and turned in the direction of Soho. It was only a fifteen-minute walk, and I used the time to consider what I should buy. Vibrators were at the forefront of my mind, because two clients had requested them and because, I supposed, they were a relatively well-known sex toy. I thought I might buy a couple, in different sizes. Also on my mental shopping list were some more condoms. I needed to find some with no taste – the lubricant on the ones I'd been using tasted absolutely disgusting, I recalled with a shudder. Surely someone must make them in a plain flavour?

I turned into the streets of Soho and soon found myself in an Ann Summers shop. I surveyed the breathtaking array of dressing-up outfits for adults: nurse, French maid, dominatrix, PVC person, seductress, take your pick. The walls were adorned with a variety of crotchless knickers, nipple tassels, whips, canes and handcuffs, and one side of the shop was dominated by a vast display of vibrators of all shapes, sizes and colours: small, large, double-ended – whatever took a person's fancy, it seemed Ann Summers could supply it.

The sales girls were not remotely embarrassed about the goods they were selling, so there was no need for me to be. I browsed for a little while, then, after much deliberation, chose two vibrators of different sizes, and a couple of pairs of pretty French knickers with matching bras. I didn't know it at the time, but these purchases represented merely the start of a growing collection of ever more adventurous sexual toys that would eventually include a cat-o'-nine-tails, thigh-high PVC boots, and a variety of gags and handcuffs. However, that day, walking back to the office with my purchases in a discreetly plain carrier bag, I felt I'd been adventurous enough. I resolved to go straight to Sarah's that night – Paul would be horrified if he found out I was in possession of a large black vibrator. I pictured the look on his face: a mix of shock and outrage. I smiled for a moment. Funny, but not that funny. Paul discovering what I was up to was a risk I didn't need to take.

My last few days as a secretary flew by, and soon – too soon – it was time for me to get ready for my first night working for Holly. I was nervous. I'd committed myself to working as an escort girl full-time, I'd given up my day job, and now I had to rise to the challenge. It was going to be much harder work than my previous escort experiences. The difference, to put it bluntly, was that this time I had to have sex with up to four clients a night, not just one. Every time I thought about that, my stomach sank with a mixture of fear and dread. I hoped I was going to be able to see this through. I knew my first night for Holly was a test – would the clients report back favourably? Would they book me again?

It was a test I had prepared for carefully – I had to pass. I showered and dressed in my new French knickers and matching bra before putting a black shift dress and jacket on top. I dried

my hair, put on make-up, and painted my long nails. I was determined that I would always look immaculate, chic and stylish, as
far removed from the classic idea of a hooker as it was possible
to get. It was a look that wasn't far from how I liked to appear;
certainly nothing that Paul would remark on. It was one way I
had of telling myself that, despite all the things I now had to do
for a living, I was still the same person I'd always been; I was still
me.

Having kissed the children goodnight, I drove to Sarah's to collect my small bag of equipment, nerves flickering in my stomach.
Then I drove to the station and took the train to Dartford. This
was where Holly had told me to meet Ant, the man who was to be
my driver.

Arriving at Dartford station, I went outside and, as instructed,
looked around for, and found, a burgundy Ford Sierra. A tall man
with a shaved head and the body of a weightlifter was leaning
against it. It had to be Ant. I walked down the pavement towards
him. He saw me coming and watched my approach with interest.

'Elizabeth?' he asked.

I nodded.

'Hi,' he said, eyeing me up and down with what I hoped was
approval. 'I'm Ant.'

We shook hands as I took in the numerous tattoos and the
several gold hoop earrings in one ear. Ant looked more like a
bouncer than a driver. We got into the car and started to chat for
a little while we waited for Trish to ring up with the first booking
and tell us where to go. Ant told me he had a long-term girlfriend

and five kids, and I quickly filled him in on my domestic situation. Then he produced a sheet of paper from the glove box.

'You've got to sign this,' he said, handing it to me.

I read it, and quickly realised it was a disclaimer of some sort.

I, the undersigned, understand that this agency, ——, is an introduction agency, and seeks to provide girls for companionship only. The agency at no time introduces people to each other with the intention that the two parties will indulge in sexual relations.

There was more of the same, spelling out the fact that I was being paid by the client for my company, and nothing else.

'Right,' I said to Ant. 'I'm off to spend an hour with someone talking about the weather, aren't I, and to be well paid for the privilege!'

We both laughed, agreeing that the laws on prostitution were archaic and absurd. As things stood, it was illegal for a man to be a pimp, but not a woman; illegal to solicit for business, but not illegal to run an escort agency advertising the company – but only the company, nothing else – of girls. It all mystified me. Why couldn't prostitution be legal? What was so very wrong with a lonely person paying for sex, if the woman providing it was happy and willing to oblige?

Just then, my phone rang. It was Trish, with the details of my first booking. I swallowed hard. The night was about to begin.

Half an hour later I was ringing the bell outside a rather smart-looking flat in Tunbridge Wells. The door opened to reveal one of the most gorgeous men I have ever seen. Six foot two, clad in tight jeans and a white T-shirt, with short, dark hair and a pair of piercing blue eyes, he looked straight out of Hollywood. Was I really being paid to sleep with this man? I hoped he couldn't read my mind.

'I'm Mick. Come in,' he smiled, revealing a set of even white teeth.

Mick poured me a drink and led me upstairs, where he peeled off his clothes to reveal, as I had suspected, the most amazing body.

I stripped down to my underwear and suggested that we begin with a massage.

Mick agreed and lay down, and off we went – two hours of the most normal sex with an extremely good-looking guy. In between, we chatted like old friends. Finally it was time to shower and go. Mick handed me the cash, thanked me, and I left.

If only all jobs could be like that one. Sleeping with Mick wasn't a hardship. Although I never got sexual pleasure from a job – I think by now I really regarded sex as something for others to enjoy – it was obviously much more pleasant to spend my time arousing and satisfying a well-mannered sex god like Mick than some smelly, overweight, rude man with bad breath. But of course they couldn't all be like Mick. While most clients weren't unpleasant, and largely wanted normal sex, they weren't the Micks of this world either. And my next booking couldn't have provided more of a contrast. I nearly fell over when a very old man opened the door. For a second I thought I must have the wrong address, but the way he smiled – semi-toothless – at me immediately told me otherwise. He was very definitely expecting me.

Jocelyn ushered me in, and I went into the bathroom to undress. While there, I noticed there was a condom floating in the loo. My mind just reeled. Had this extremely elderly gentleman – Jocelyn was somewhere in his eighties, I suspected – already had sex at least once this evening? The mind boggled. Was he some kind of sex-mad old-age pensioner? A sex maniac with a free bus pass?

I walked back into the bedroom in just my red underwear, to find Jocelyn already naked on the bed. I winced inwardly at the sight of his body. Gravity had not been kind – his flesh hung limply off his frame. I felt a stab of pity towards him, a softening of my heart. We would all be old one day.

'Massage?' I suggested.

I had my procedure down to a fine art. My thoughts were racing as I got on with the job. Jocelyn might be older than my usual client, but he was still a man, and all the signs were there to indicate that he was already responding. What did it matter if I was about to sleep with a man old enough to be my grandfather? He seemed clean enough, and I couldn't afford to be picky; I was in this job to save my family and had to take whatever clients came my way. And why shouldn't old people be allowed to enjoy sex, anyway? Why should it just be a young person's pleasure? In my limited experience, it was becoming clear to me that most men loved sex, regardless of their shape, size and age. It was only in the world of movies that you had to be drop-dead gorgeous to get laid.

Back in the car again, I felt exhausted and ready for home. But there was no chance of that – I was only halfway through my night. Ant, turning on the engine, told me we already had another booking. My heart plummeted. I just wanted to go home. Buck up, I told myself fiercely. This is what you signed up for. Let's just get on with it.

'Okay,' I said to Ant, getting out my make-up compact to tidy up a little. 'Where are we off to now?'

It was past midnight by now, and with two clients behind me, I was worried that I might be starting to look a little worn. I'd washed before leaving both clients, but still, I had slept with two men. I looked at myself in my compact mirror for a moment; then I put on some lipstick and ran a comb through my hair.

Too soon, Ant was drawing into the kerb once again.

'Do I look all right, Ant?' I asked somewhat doubtfully, before stepping out of the car.

'You look great, love.'

'Sure?'

Ant looked at me with something like amazement on his face. 'Honestly, darling, you don't need to worry. Some of the other girls look really rough and they don't worry at all. But you look lovely, and what do you do – you worry! Trust me, you don't need to. You look fine.'

'Thanks, Ant,' I said, refusing to wonder what the other girls looked like. I knew by now there were all sorts in this business – the penniless young immigrant type, like the beautiful Russian I'd met at Jimmy's; the junkie feeding her habit, as so often represented by the papers; the middle-class mother type, like me.

As I walked up the path to client number three, I was grateful for the vote of confidence. It really wasn't easy to maintain a positive self-image in this job.

Client number three was a thirtysomething birthday boy rounding off a night out with a present to himself – me. He was jolly and happy and delighted to see me. Once again I swung into my routine, and an hour later was closing the door on another satisfied client. I'd massaged, and sucked, and licked and fucked. I was definitely earning my cash – and my purse was starting to bulge with notes, which was the whole point of the exercise. I felt relief flood through me as I realised that so far tonight I'd taken care of the outstanding house insurance, the electricity bill and two months of council tax arrears. I knew as I got back in the car that if Holly had another client for me, I'd do it before calling it a night and heading home. That way, I could do our supermarket shop on Saturday without worrying. I might even let Alice have the shop-bought fairy cakes she was desperate for, and Alexander the batteries he needed for his Action Man torch.

'Right, Ant, what's next?' I said determinedly as I climbed back into the car.

The next job was a bit of a drive, so I sat back, pulled my diary out of my handbag, and started to make a list of all the things I had to do tomorrow.

Things to Remember:
Sports kit for Alexander
Present for Charlotte to take to party after school

Appointment with Alice's form teacher – 3.30 p.m.

Bake fairy cakes for school sale

Emily – cooking class – take eggs and flour—

'Oh hell,' I said aloud. How could I have forgotten to buy the ingredients Emily needed?

'What's the matter?' Ant looked at me in the rear-view mirror.

'My eldest daughter has a cooking class tomorrow,' I groaned. 'She has to take in a packet of self-raising flour and a dozen eggs and I've forgotten to buy them.'

Forgetting things was unlike me, I was generally highly organised. With six children, I had to be. It must have been because I was so preoccupied with preparing for my first night with Holly. But I could hardly tell Emily that; all I knew was that she was going to be very upset. Like all kids, she just wanted her school life to go smoothly, to have the right things when she needed them. Now I had let her down.

With another glance in the rear-view mirror, Ant took in my deepening frown. 'There's a twenty-four-hour Tesco's coming up,' he suggested.

'Oh, could we?' I said, leaping at the suggestion.

And so, at 1.30 a.m., on the way to my fourth client of the night, we made a short detour, and I nipped into the supermarket and dashed up the aisles with my basket to the baking section to get the things Emily needed. While I was there, I chucked in a packet of hundreds and thousands, which I needed for the fairy cakes I was making for the monthly school cake stall being held this Friday, and some baking powder. I knew we were running low at home. On the way to the checkout, I passed through toiletries. Might as well add a few condoms while I'm here, I thought, putting in several packets in all textures and flavours. What a mixed bag my life was.

A few minutes later, I climbed back into the car with several shopping bags.

'You're just like my girlfriend,' Ant said, eyeing the bags with a grin. 'Physically unable to go to a supermarket and buy just the things she went for!'

Then he stepped on it a bit, to make up the time we had lost.

I sat back, looking out at the dark streets we were travelling through, happy that Emily was going to have the things she needed for her cooking lesson, after all. Now I just had this last job to get through, then I could go home.

Twenty minutes later, Ant pulled up outside the home of client number four. We both read the sign above the door in silence. It was a funeral parlour. Oh great. I was about to have sex with an undertaker. Whatever next?

'Are you sure this is right, Ant?' I asked.

Ant double-checked the address. 'Yup.'

'Okay,' I sighed, and got out of the car. I walked over and rang the bell.

'Hello,' I said brightly to the man who answered the door. He had a thin, pale face and – was I imagining it? – a rather mournful air. We went upstairs, to his flat.

'I live above the shop,' he explained, a little unnecessarily.

'So I see,' I said, undressing briskly.

I couldn't help it. As I bounced up and down on him, I found my thoughts turning to the corpses that surely lay downstairs awaiting their day of burial. If there was an afterlife, what did their spirits think of what was going on a few floors above their discarded mortal forms? Whether I believed in an afterlife or not, there was no getting away from it: I was having sex with a man in a house containing God knew how many dead bodies. Spooky. Think of what it's doing for us, I told myself wearily, moving up and down on the undertaker's cock. I pictured the kitchen drawer slowly getting emptier; I imagined no longer being afraid to answer the front door in case it was the bailiffs; I saw myself at the repossession hearing to be held next week confidently telling the judge that I now had a night job and could guarantee large monthly payments if he gave me one more chance.

The undertaker came with a gasp: 'Yes! Yes!'

Hurray. Wouldn't be long till I was home now. And though my body ached and my eyes were dry with tiredness, I knew my night out had been worth it.

The results were in within a couple of days: two of the four clients had called the agency and asked for me again and my first night with Holly was deemed to be a success. Apparently this was a high rate of repeat business, and the agency were pleased with me.

After that, the bookings came thick and fast. Just as Holly had told me, she had clients coming out of her ears. I'll never forget that first week at Holly's. By the second or third day I'd realised how gentle my introduction to the escort world had been with Jimmy – just one booking a night, with a maximum of two a week. Now that I was seeing clients all night long, it was a huge shock to the system, and within days I was absolutely shattered.

There was quite a lot of travelling involved. Holly's agency took bookings from quite a broad geographical area. In my first week I had bookings as far-flung as Milton Keynes and Oxford. This meant that sometimes I didn't get home until five or so in the morning. In those early days I thanked my lucky stars for Ant, my wonderful driver. It made my packed nightlife much easier. I didn't have to worry about getting lost, or running out of petrol, or staying awake enough to drive. Ant did all that. I was free to nap between jobs, or, as I often did, chat to Ant about all sorts of things.

However tired I was, I didn't dare to turn a booking down. I'd said at the outset that I wanted to work as much as possible, and I was determined to live up to my word. As with Jimmy, I was fearful that if I turned down a booking, Trish would think I didn't have what it took and start giving the jobs to other girls. It might be completely exhausting, but it was having the desired result. I was earning £400 a night, several nights a week, the debts were steadily reducing, and I was also covering our daily outgoings so we didn't build up any more. However physically and emotionally demanding those first days were, I just forced myself to carry on. It would all be worth it, I told myself. We were nowhere near out of the woods. I still had the biggest hurdle to come: the repossession hearing.

I didn't work the night before the hearing, so that I would be awake and alert when it was my turn to make our case. I knew that even though Paul was coming with me, the talking would be down to me.

The morning of the repossession hearing came. I felt sick with nerves as I went through the usual early morning routine. I gave the children breakfast and automatically started to fill the lunch boxes while my thoughts raced ahead. Would I be standing in my kitchen this time tomorrow, knowing that we were on borrowed time, that the house was no longer ours? I looked at my children sitting round the table. Victoria was still half asleep, Alexander's hair was standing up on end where he'd slept on it; all the kids were eating their Shreddies, munching their toast, drinking their orange juice; it was our usual daily scene, and I didn't want it to stop. I felt myself stiffen with resolve. I was getting good at fighting battles, at solving our problems, I told myself. I had to be able to sort this one out, too, I just had to. Surely it would have to be a very unreasonable judge who wouldn't give me another chance?

Three hours later, I was standing in front of the stern-looking district judge, neat in my navy work suit, setting out my case for keeping our family home.

'I'm now in the position to make regular monthly payments,' I told him in what I hoped was a confident manner. 'I've changed to a well-paid night job, which also means that my childminding costs are down. That money can now be redirected to the mortgage, as can the increase in my wage.'

The judge looked down at me thoughtfully.

'It is also our family home and has been for some time, sir,' I added. 'I have six children, and it would be terrible to disrupt them all, now that I'm in a situation when I can pay the mortgage. If we lose our home, there's no certainty that the council would be able to house us near my children's schools, and so losing our home could disrupt their education as well.'

I stopped, breathless, and waited.

I don't know if it was this last plea – perhaps he had children or grandchildren who had fallen on hard times? – or the facts, but after a further moment of thought, he had decided.

'I give you three months,' he said. In that time I had to make the regular payments I had promised. A further hearing would be booked in for three months' time. If I had not made the payments, the building society would then have the right to repossess our house.

I beamed at the judge with relief, my body swaying slightly as the tension that had been holding me upright flooded out of me.

'Oh, thank you, your honour,' I said. 'Thank you so much.' I could have kissed him.

We filed out of the courtroom. Paul, who had uttered not a word, strode ahead of me.

The euphoria at saving our home stayed with me as I went back to work that night, but even though I knew how the money I now earned was literally changing our lives, it was still hard leaving. I hated leaving the children, the cosiness; hated getting dressed up for hours of pretending to be someone I wasn't. Every night, I longed to stay at home, but knew I couldn't.

At least I had come up with a plan that meant I was able to look after the children myself. The agency was pleased with the number of repeat bookings I was getting, and so I was able to negotiate with them as to the hours I worked. I had asked Trish if I could start each night at about 9.30 p.m, which meant that I was at home for most of the evening, and could ensure the kids were in bed by the time I left. This at least gave me some peace of mind.

I'd leave home with a heavy heart, though. There weren't many nights when I didn't think, Have I really got to go? even though I knew the answer only too well. The answer lay in the red bills still queuing to be paid, in the postponed repossession order, in the school fees overdue, the mountainous debts on our credit cards. So every night, I'd get dressed, kiss my children, and leave, closing the door quietly behind me, wishing the next few hours away so I could be back.

Soon after the repossession hearing, I had sat down and addressed the issue of the backlog of our debts. One by one, I'd rung up our creditors – the electricity company, the local council, the credit card operators and so on – and told them that I was now in a position to start making regular monthly payments, and if they would give me the time, obviously this would eventually lead to the whole debt being cleared. Since this avoided the expense and bother of legal action, they'd all agreed, and I had set up a number of direct debits to make sure payments didn't get overlooked. I had based the payments on what I knew I could earn if I worked five or six nights a week, most weeks of the year. I'd left myself enough over to pay the daily expenses, and to save for the periodic bills that landed every now and then, such as the school fees, tax bills and Victoria's ongoing health bills.

Almost every penny I earned was going on the essentials of life, but occasionally I would allow us a treat, and buy the children something special. For years they had been clamouring for a dog. While I'd been away from home all day working, I hadn't felt we could manage one, but things had changed – I was at home all day – and this was a change the children had picked up on. Now I was regularly besieged by their pleas of 'Oh, please, Mummy, can't we have a dog? Pleeeease! We'd help look after it, really we would.'

I had given it some thought, and had decided that a dog would be a good addition to our household. It would be good for the children to take some of the responsibility for it, helping with the walking and feeding. And I knew that if I chose wisely, a friendly, happy dog would be fun for them to have around. So when I learned that a friend of a friend's Labrador had had a litter, on impulse I put our name on the list, without telling the children. Then I promptly forgot all about it and got on with our lives.

About six weeks later, the call came. The puppy was now eight weeks old. It was a male, as I'd requested, it had had all its injections, and it was now awaiting collection. I swallowed hard and said I'd be over later in the day.

That afternoon, I set off for the farm where the puppy had been born. I stopped at the pet shop in our town and bought a bed, a lead, some food, a dog bowl and a book on dog training. Then I drove on to collect the puppy, berating myself all the way. What a stupid thing to do! What had I let myself in for, aside from more bills and one more living thing to care for? As if I didn't have enough going on in my life!

These thoughts were banished the moment I saw the black Labrador puppy sitting patiently waiting for me. All his brothers and sisters had already gone to their new homes, and when I tentatively went towards him, he padded over to me and nuzzled my hand with his wet little nose as if to say, 'I knew all along you'd come.' He was the smallest of the litter, the owner told me, and his tail wasn't quite straight; was I sure he was right for us? Perfectly, I told the owner, writing out the cheque and handing it over before she could change her mind about letting us have him. She pocketed it, scooped up the wriggling puppy and put him into a cardboard box she had waiting.

'What are you going to call him?' she asked, as we carried the box to the car.

'Scooby,' I replied. For some reason I'd known it the minute I'd seen him. I had a feeling this was going to be a scampering, happy, slightly silly dog, a dog that got up to a few tricks. Scooby, after that lunatic dog Scooby Doo in the children's favourite cartoon series, seemed a very apt name for him.

I took Scooby home and settled him in the kitchen on his new bed. I couldn't wait for the children to come home and see him –

they were being dropped by a friend that day. Finally, the kids stamped into the kitchen as they did every afternoon after school, heading directly for the fridge in search of glasses of milk and cheese strings and yoghurts to keep them going till teatime.

'Mind where you tread, kids,' I said, smiling. 'Don't squash the dog.'

Scooby, who had been snuffling round the kitchen on the trail of interesting smells, now leapt up to meet them, wagging his tail in greeting, licking their hands and sniffing round their feet; now, I noticed, he was chewing one of the laces in Alexander's shoes. He'd already demolished one of my slippers.

'A puppy!' Victoria shrieked in delight, a smile flashing across her features.

'A puppy!' the rest of the children chorused together, taking the reality of Scooby in and crowding round him.

Scooby, showing all the signs that he was going to survive well in our household, didn't seem to mind the crowd at all; in fact he seemed to be relishing the attention, leaping up at the children and barking his puppy-bark.

'What's he called, Mummy?' Charlotte asked.

'Scooby,' I told them all, grinning from ear to ear. I could see already that he was a good addition to the family.

I was finding seeing several clients a night very tiring. It didn't take me long to work out that there was a way to make my life a great deal easier while still earning as much cash: by building up some clients who booked to see me regularly. Trish had told me that in general, a 'regular' – someone who booked to see the same girl, often – was likely to book for a longer period, to pay more, and to give a good tip. Quite often a girl could get the same sum of money doing just one job with a regular as she could get from doing four jobs with strangers. Trish had told me stories about regular clients paying a girl £1000 or more just to stay the night.

This sounded very attractive to me; and by this time, my confidence in my capability as an escort girl was growing. It was as if I'd served my apprenticeship. The early doubts, fears and embarrassments had all been dispelled. Much as I disliked my work, I knew I was now getting rather good at what I did, and I hoped it was only a matter of time before I had an encounter with a client that led to a regular appointment.

This happened one Saturday night a couple of weeks later. Trish sent me to a man called Eric. Ant drove me, and before long we were pulling up in front of a beautiful town house overlooking the sea. Stepping out of the car, I collected my little bag from the boot and told Ant I'd see him in two hours.

Eric ushered me inside, and, as I admired his house he told me that he was a single dad with children in their early teens. I could see them smiling out of photographs on the hall table.

We went upstairs to the bedroom, and, sitting down in a chair, Eric asked me if I had any red underwear. Reaching for my bag of tricks I told him that I did and would just go and slip it on. I nipped into the bathroom and put on my matching red bra and panties, red suspender belt and stockings, and my black high heels. How far I had come from those early days of easy embarrassment, I thought wryly, as I walked out towards Eric with barely a flicker of self-consciousness.

Eric clearly liked what he saw if the growing bulge in his trousers was anything to go by. He sat back in a chair and asked me if I had any red lipstick. 'Bright red,' he added.

'Yes,' I said, turning to my bag once again.

'Put it on in front of me,' he begged. 'Kneel in front of me and put it on. Lots of it.'

I did as he asked, applying a thick layer of red lipstick to my mouth, and looking back at him rather poutily. Eric just looked at me as if he was hypnotised. After a little while, he undid his trousers and his cock sprang out.

'Suck me,' he begged. 'Suck me hard, leaving your lipstick on my cock.'

I inched forward on my knees, and quickly rolled on a condom. Then I took his cock in my mouth and began to work it. I sucked hard as it slid in and out of my mouth. Suddenly Eric pushed my head up.

'Stop,' he panted. 'Make me wait.'

So I sat back again, and he looked at me rather feverishly for a while. I decided to pass the time applying a little more red lipstick, ever so slowly, looking at him as I did so. I knelt up in front of him again, slowly pulling back his trousers and trailing my long red fingernails idly up and down his naked thighs. Finally, it was as if he was in some kind of agony and could stand it no longer. He pushed his legs wide and thrust his cock out at me again.

I knew what he wanted. I moved forward, and took his cock in one hand. Slowly, ever so slowly, maintaining our eye contact as long as I could, I lowered my head to his cock. Then I parted my red lips and took him in my mouth again. I could feel the effort he was making to hold on. Before thirty seconds had passed, he'd pushed me off again. He looked at me for a moment, panting. Then he stood up and crossed the room to the bed, where he lay down.

'Climb on top of me,' he said, and I followed him to the bed and straddled him. We continued like that for a little while, and then Eric said, 'I want to take you from behind.'

I slid off, and knelt on all fours in front of him. I helped him slide his prick into me, and we fucked again, Eric panting and moaning. I really couldn't believe he had far to go, but it seemed he had one change of position left in him. He pulled out of me and said, 'Roll over on to your back.'

I did, and once again Eric slid into me, this time with him lying on top of me. As he worked to a climax, I opened my eyes and looked at him. He was too lost in himself now for me to need to pretend I was enjoying myself. With a final shout he came, and, after a few more short thrusts, collapsed on to the bed.

'Did you enjoy that?' he asked finally, his breathing back to normal.

'Oh yes,' I replied swiftly, without a qualm. This wasn't the truth – I was there for the money – but it was obviously what he wanted to hear. I'd come to realise that nearly all clients hoped that I enjoyed the sex, and sometimes writhing around in indication that you were having a marvellous time wasn't enough. They had to ask. And if they did, I always said yes as convincingly as I could. Making them feel like studs was part of the job.

'Eric,' I said, 'it was fantastic.'

He smiled at me with real satisfaction and asked if he could book me again for the same time next week.

An hour later, I was home. I climbed the stairs quietly and peeped in on the children: Emily, I noted, was safely back from her night out with her friends, clothes thrown all over the floor; Alice's side of the room was hardly any tidier; Jack was snoring in his cot, the legacy of a recent cold; Alexander was completely invisible under the duvet. Victoria and Charlotte looked like twins under their matching pink Groovy Chicks duvets. With everyone accounted for, I continued along the corridor to my bedroom. I quickly undressed, pulled on my favourite old flannel nightdress, and crawled under the duvet next to Paul's silent form. It was after two in the morning, and I was bone tired. Even though it was Sunday the next day, I would still be up early, as every parent of small children knows. I closed my eyes tight and willed myself to sleep. I calculated that if I fell asleep that very second, I could get the best part of five hours.

Of course, I found myself wide awake, my thoughts racing ahead to Sunday morning. We were going to watch Alexander in his rugby match, and I'd offered to help cook the bacon sandwiches in the club house. Had I remembered to buy a new jar of hot chocolate? Everyone liked a mugful after the game was over. I'd have to check in the morning. I loved going to cheer Alexander on. He was a good player, and to boost his slightly wobbly confidence I usually bribed him to just go for it, with a five-pound reward for every try he scored. Last week he'd scored two, despite the hindrance of Scooby, who'd tried to join in the game, running on to the pitch and chasing the ball. The referee had had to blow his whistle and bring the game to a halt, while I sheepishly retrieved Scooby and persuaded Emily to take him for a walk on his lead. Alexander had been mortified. This week, I decided drowsily, my eyelids heavy at last, it would be better for Scooby to stay at home.

Chapter Seven

*E*ric proved to be just the first on my list of regulars. Now I quickly began to acquire several more. One afternoon, not long after my first meeting with Eric, Holly rang me to say she had a client who wanted a longer than standard booking, from about 6 p.m. to 1 a.m. She told me the gentleman wanted a girl he could take to the theatre and out for supper before adjourning to his hotel. She'd thought of me, she said, because the reports came back that as well as being good at my job, I was also presentable and interesting to talk to. I laughed at this, and supposed that if the competition was anything like the girl I'd met at Jimmy's – stunning, but with only three words of English – this didn't necessarily say anything particularly wonderful about me. However, the thought of being spared the sexual needs of four or five individuals in one night meant I took the job willingly.

I glanced at my watch: it was 1.30 p.m. Leaving so early for work meant I had to get a little ahead of myself. I rang Paul, and he agreed to come home earlier than usual to look after the children. Then I took a chicken casserole I'd made the week before out of the freezer and put it in the microwave to defrost. I scored and pricked several potatoes for baking, and turned on the oven. I set the table, and went to the laundry room to check the washing. Alice was playing in a hockey match the next day and needed a clean games shirt and skirt.

Some hours later, with Paul home and the children all happily having their tea, I dressed for work and took the train to London to meet the unknown client, Rory, at the appointed bar.

I had never met a client in a bar before – I was to look out for a man in a tweed jacket with the *Daily Telegraph* under his right arm – and hoped that the meeting part would go smoothly. I didn't fancy a wasted evening with no client and no money.

I approached the bar, which was empty apart from one grey-haired man in a brown tweed jacket. I examined him discreetly. No *Daily Telegraph*. I looked around. There were a number of couples murmuring to each other over their after-work drinks, but no other single men. I pulled out a bar stool, sat down on it and glanced back at the man in the brown jacket. We made eye contact and he immediately came over.

'Are you meeting somebody?' he asked.

I looked at him speculatively. Could this be him?

'Yes,' I replied cautiously.

'Rory?' he suggested.

I smiled. 'Yes. You are . . . Rory?' I asked, and he smiled back, nodding.

'I'm Elizabeth,' I said.

I sat back on my bar stool to study him while he ordered me a drink. He was in his mid-fifties, I guessed, quite lean and fit-looking, with closely cropped grey hair. His accent clearly indicated that he hailed from up North.

I watched intently as my drink was poured, something I always did now since Simon's words of warning.

Drinks in hand, we began to chat. I quickly discovered that Rory's family owned a business. He told me he came to London regularly on business trips. I silently surmised that he used these trips for a bit of London life coupled with some recreational sex.

Now Rory was reaching into his pocket.

'Have you seen *Starlight Express*?' he asked, producing two tickets.

I shook my head. 'But I'd love to. I adore musicals,' I said truthfully.

Rory smiled back. I relaxed. I could tell the evening was going to be a success.

Rory was a typical West End tourist. He wasn't in London often, so when he was he went for the big names to be sure of a good experience. After *Starlight Express* we dined at a well-known restaurant in Soho as if we were old friends, chatting easily about the show and books we'd both read before returning to his extremely smart hotel. It was already nearly midnight. 'My wife has arrived,' Rory said smoothly as he signed me in. I nearly leapt out of my skin – an irate wife, that was all I needed – before I realised he meant me.

Neither the concierge nor the bellboy turned a hair.

'Welcome, Mrs——' they beamed at me, taking my suitcase. 'We'll have this sent to your room immediately.'

I thanked them as if I stayed in five-star hotels all week long, and followed Rory to the lifts.

Once in his room, Rory continued to treat me as if I really was his much-loved wife. He hung up my jacket in the cupboard and asked if I wanted anything from the minibar. Then he disappeared into the bathroom and re-emerged a few moments later in a white bathrobe. He lay back on the bed, arms behind his head.

'I might just slip a few things off too,' I said, looking at him suggestively from under my fringe. I began to undress, revealing my skimpy underwear. His eyes were like saucers. I decided to keep up the 'wife' thing, as this was so obviously what he was after. I went round to his side of the bed, and perched my bottom on the edge, my back to him.

'I can't seem to manage the clip on my bra – could you possibly help me, Rory?' I asked.

Rory sounded a little hoarse as he said yes, certainly he'd try. He undid the clip and I turned back towards him, my breasts bare.

He reached his hands up and cupped them. I'd got used to men wanting to touch me by now, and it didn't bother me any more.

'What would you like me to do?' I asked throatily. 'You just let me know, Rory. I'm all yours.'

It was a straightforward romp that took place on the crisp hotel sheets that night. I'd noticed at dinner that Rory was a rather traditional, meat and two veg man, and wasn't surprised to find that his sexual appetites followed along similar lines. I was almost surprised that he didn't ask me to turn the lights out. When he was ready, I rolled a condom on to him, and Rory, bearing his weight on his elbows in gentlemanly fashion in order not to squash me, pushed himself into me and hunched his buttocks. He started to thrust, in and out and in and out, and I resisted the urge to look at the ceiling. Instead I closed my eyes, and moaned softly.

'Oh. Oh yes,' I said. 'Oh yes, that's really good.'

Encouraged, Rory went faster and faster, like a train gathering pace, until, with a straining sound, he ejaculated.

'Aaaaah,' he said. Then, after a few moments, 'God, that was good, love. Just what the doctor ordered.'

An hour later, I left the hotel a thousand pounds richer and with a beautiful pale blue woollen scarf in my bag.

'It's a little something for you,' Rory had said, pressing it on me. 'When we next meet I'll bring you a nice cardigan. Something to keep out the autumn chill, my dear.'

I'd thanked him and kissed him on the cheek, promising to make myself free for him next time he was in town. Outside, across the street, in the chill early morning, Ant was waiting to take me home.

I suppose it was inevitable that I'd meet a wider variety of clients, working as hard as I now was. Just by the law of averages, I was likely to run into someone who wanted something a little more outlandish sooner or later.

Midway through a night's work, I rang in to the agency for details of my next booking. Trish was working that night, and told me I was to go to Bicester, to see a client the agency had worked with before. Ant and I set off, and an hour later I was knocking on the door.

The guy who opened it was wearing a weird get-up of tight leather shirt and shorts, rather like Russell Crowe wore in *Gladiator*. He couldn't get me into the house quickly enough, telling me he was really pleased to see me. I smiled at him, slightly uncertain.

'That's nice,' I said.

But my words were lost on him. He was already leading me through to the sitting room. There, in front of the three-piece suite, was a bench that had clearly been designed for a particular purpose. It had loads of straps and buckles on it, and next to it lay a large black vibrator. Taking all this in with a glance, I had no time to worry about what I was going to be asked to do, as the client, beside himself with excitement, began to tell me: he spoke fast, words tumbling out of him as if he could barely wait to begin. I was to strap him down and buckle him up. Then I was to push the vibrator up his bottom and go. As he explained all this, he handed over £200 and whipped off his leather pants. Then, pulling on a hood, he bent over the bench, arse in the air, waiting expectantly.

What could I do? Pocketing the money, I quickly buckled him up, his legs wide apart. Then I picked up the vibrator, turned it on, and gently eased it into him, as he panted with pleasure.

I stood back for a moment and took in the scene. The man was now securely strapped down, with a vibrator buzzing away in his bottom. He was moaning slightly in what I assumed was ecstasy. The whole thing had taken less than ten minutes, and my part in the exercise was at an end. But one thing bothered me: how on earth was he going to get out of this set-up? He didn't want me to wait – he'd made that quite clear, so after one last doubtful glance in his direction, I turned and left. But I couldn't dismiss him so easily from my mind. I got back into the car and sat in silence for a moment. Would the man be all right?

'Ant, you won't believe what just happened in there,' I said, and told him the whole story.

Ant doubled up in laughter, and told me not to worry, the guy very probably knew what he was doing. But I couldn't help feeling uneasy. I decided to ring the agency before we moved on, just to double-check I wasn't supposed to wait.

'Trish,' I began, and quickly explained the problem. Trish listened, and then she, too, fell about laughing. When she finally pulled herself together, she explained, 'Don't worry, love, he's a regular with the agency and he always wants the same thing. He'll be absolutely fine.'

I took her word for it, and, having given Ant and Trish a laugh at my innocence, I set off with Ant for our next booking.

Working for Holly, I began to shed much of my naivety. I realised how much of an illusion life really was. I learned that people were rarely what they seemed.

I was well aware that this could be applied to me as much as anyone I met through my work. As I dashed about in my sweater, jeans and boots doing the school run every day before making a large shepherd's pie for tea and a batch of fairy cakes for the school cake stall held on the last Friday of every month, I was just a mum. I took Alice to pony club, cheered Alexander on in his rugby match, took Victoria to her check-up with the ear doctor. Little did the other mothers or teachers know that at night I was forced to metamorphose into another being entirely, to don stockings and suspenders and have sex for a living. The two lives I was living were closely intertwined, and I very much hoped that they would never collide.

To some extent, all my clients were living a double life too; it was just a question of degree. While many wanted to take me out to dinner and pretend I was their girlfriend, there was always a minority who wanted something quite other. For every ten straightforward clients, there was one who had a different play in mind. That kind of client wanted to act out their sexual fantasy, whatever that might be, and had hired me to help them make it seem real. Over the next few months, as I worked all night long, six nights a week, this happened time and again.

One evening, I went as directed to a very smart hotel in Knightsbridge for a booking of several hours with a man called Dash. Holly had rung me with the details that afternoon, and the only indication that I might be in for anything less than a routine job was that she had asked me what my shoe size was. I didn't spare this unusual question much thought, but merely accepted the job.

I walked through the lobby of the hotel in my usual smart dark suit, high heels clicking authoritatively on the marble floor. I breezed past the concierge as if I lived there and took the lift up to the right floor. I walked along to Dash's room, knocked on the door and waited. Within seconds it was opened by a tall, dark-skinned man who, I immediately observed, was naked except for a long shoe lace, which was tied round his waist and also tied between his legs. His penis, flaccid, dangled down between the laces. On his feet were a pair of high-heeled black satin shoes decorated with diamonds..

Lucky I'm not room service, I thought. They'd drop the tray in shock.

I introduced myself, smiling, hoping my face betrayed nothing of my amazement.

'I am Dash,' said the vision, in a Latin drawl. 'Please, come in.'

I noticed as I walked in that there was a pile of cocaine on one of the side tables. A credit card lay beside it. Obviously Dash had already got stuck in to his evening of recreation.

Dash asked me to undress down to my underwear, leaving my shoes on, and to come and sit in a chair. I did as he asked. He came to kneel in front of me, still in his bizarre get-up, and picked up one of my ankles as gently as if he were holding the Holy Grail. Lovingly, worshipfully, he began to kiss around my ankle and the top of my foot. Slowly, as if he was teasing himself, he undid the straps of my shoes and took them off, one by one. He put a line of coke in one of my shoes and licked it out. Then he took his shoes off and put them on my feet.

'Beautiful,' he sighed, in apparent ecstasy. He didn't seem to mind that they were a little large for me. He pulled me to my feet, and together, as if we were lovers in the park, we strolled around the room, holding hands, Dash smiling with delight at the sight of his shoes on my feet.

After a while, he led me over to a cupboard. He threw open the door to reveal several more pairs of shoes, all obviously extremely expensive and fashionable. Dash had clearly beaten a path down Bond Street, returning home heavily laden with a wide selection.

He sat me down again and proceeded to bring over the shoes, pair by pair, and fit them on my feet. It was like a bizarre version of Cinderella, except that there was no handsome prince in sight. All the shoes fitted me perfectly. As the cogs whirred in my brain, I realised that this wasn't coincidence – he had obviously bought all the shoes that afternoon once Holly had given him my shoe size. They must have cost £300 a pair, and there were at least ten pairs. Dash, I concluded, took his shoe fetish very seriously indeed.

All the while, he was slipping shoes on and off my feet, and in between licking cocaine out of the insides of them. His eyes were very glittery and his penis rose above his string belt like a tower. I could tell he was reaching the end of his control. By now I was wearing a beautiful pair of red crocodile-skin stilettoes. Dash, meanwhile, had crammed his feet into my shoes.

'Come,' he said, mincing towards the bed.

He's going to get terrible blisters, I thought as I crossed the room. I lay down, as he indicated, on my back, shoes, needless to say, still on my feet. He carefully laid out a line of cocaine on my stomach and snorted it before sprinkling more of the powder around the edges of my pussy. Licking it off, he told me he was ready.

I rolled on a condom, and he was inside. Just as I was wondering whether there was a hope in hell of him coming with so much coke in him, he groaned and panted, and it was all over.

All this had taken hours. It was almost time for me to go. I showered and dressed and was about to put my shoes back on when Dash stopped me.

'Please, couldn't I keep your shoes?' he begged, as if they were the crown jewels rather than a pair from Shoe Express.

'Well, yes, but what shall I go home in?' I asked.

Dash gestured towards the many pairs now spread all over the room. 'Take your pick,' he said. I did, and went home £500 richer with a beautiful pair of black satin, pearl-encrusted Jimmy Choos on my feet.

Dash became one of my regulars when he was in town. My collection of evening shoes with impossible heels swelled, and I quickly discovered that, as strange sexual fantasies go, his was pretty harmless and easy to accommodate.

By now, the aspect of my new life with which I struggled the most wasn't the sex. That could be disgusting at worst, bearable at best, but by focusing on the reason why I was doing it and what that meant for my family, I could get through it, although of course I had my low moments, when I really battled with what I was making myself do. What I was really struggling with now were the lies that being an escort girl involved.

I have always regarded the truth as extremely important, and until all this had been a very truthful person. Yet suddenly I was lying to everyone around me. I lied on a daily basis to Paul. I was lying to the children. And I was lying to many of my friends. If we went to a dinner party, I lied about what I did. If mothers at school asked me about work, I told them all about my invented job at a word-processing centre, and the raft of fictitious friends who worked with me.

Lying isn't something I'm very good at, and I don't feel comfortable doing it. I remember one rare evening off from work, when I went out for supper in a local Chinese restaurant with Sarah and two other close friends, all of whom knew what I did for a living. We really had fun that night, and coming home a couple of hours later I remember wondering why I had enjoyed myself so much. It suddenly dawned on me that it was because I didn't have to tell any lies. Those three close, supportive friends all knew exactly what I was up to. I didn't have to mention 'Diane', my fictitious boss at the word-processing centre, or describe the hell of my train journey to my imaginary job. I could just be me. There weren't many people I could do that with any more, and I had temporarily forgotten what it felt like.

Feeling as I did about lying, it was ironic, then, that, unable to help myself, I had started a whole new set of lies on top of the ones about my work, making my life even more complicated. Without noticing it, I had fallen in love.

David and I had become ever closer during our daily commutes while I was still working at the law firm, as we traded problems and offered each other sympathy. Towards the end of my time there, I had known that my feelings for him were changing from friendship to something deeper. I didn't want them to – life was more than complicated enough. I had six children to love and keep. I simply didn't have any time to fall in love.

But, as everyone knows, matters of the heart don't respond to reason. And when David, who lived round the corner from us, told me that he missed our shared journeys, I found myself admitting that so did I. And when David kissed me, I found myself kissing him back.

From then on, we snatched a few hours together every couple of weeks. It wasn't much, but then there wasn't much opportunity. I was either working or looking after my children, and David still lived with his girlfriend and their son, but every few weeks we would manage to meet for supper and spend a few hours together. In between, we would speak every day.

My affair with David meant there were even more people to lie to, and even more lies to tell. I was lying to David about what I did for a living. I didn't tell him because I just didn't think he'd understand. What man would, for God's sake? So from the start, I told him the usual story about the night job at the word-processing centre. I would call him in the evenings, when I was in between clients, and he'd ask me what I was doing.

'Oh, I'm by the photocopier copying some documents,' I'd say, inventing wildly. I couldn't tell him the truth – that I was on my way to some smart surburban house in Esher, very probably to give my third blow job of the evening.

Inwardly I winced at every lie, and David remembered every detail I gave him. I should have been flattered that he was so interested in me, but it made life more complicated, because it meant that to be convincing I had to remember every detail too. I was used to Paul asking me nothing, or, on the rare occasions he did ask, not listening to the answers I'd given him. David was different. He'd often ask me how Diane was, until it got to the point that I'd built up the image of a person with a whole range of characteristics and experiences, a family and a boyfriend. He asked about my other work colleagues, too, until I'd invented a whole set of people. I wanted it to stop. I hated it all, but the lies just spiralled. They developed a life all of their own; they just got worse and worse.

Despite this, I couldn't let go of David. He gave me something too precious. He made me feel special. At a time when I was drowning in a sea of cash-for-sex encounters, he showed me that I was a woman worth cherishing. Being with David reminded me that, despite the nature of my work life, I was still the woman I'd always been; underneath the suspenders and the sexual knowhow, I was still me, a woman with a head full of romantic notions, able to love and desire a man in his own right, for himself, no cash required. Being with him reminded me that I was still capable of falling in love.

I hadn't forgotten the advice of Mark, my very first client, on how important it was to look after my health, including getting myself checked regularly for sexual diseases. Suddenly, amazingly, I'd been working for three months, and I knew it was high time I went and got myself checked.

I knew there was a drop-in clinic attached to Dartford Hospital where you could turn up and get a full sexual health check-up. I drove there early one afternoon, leaving myself enough time before I had to collect the children from school – we were all going on to the birthday party of a family friend. I was rather dreading it. I knew I was going to have to tell the nurses what I was up to – there was no point in going if I wasn't honest, as they wouldn't test me for the right things – and I hoped they weren't going to make me feel bad about it.

They couldn't have been nicer. When my turn came, a nurse ushered me into a room and asked me what my job was. I blurted it out, and she didn't miss a beat.

'Oh, you're a prostitute, darling, okay, that's fine. Nice to see you're looking after yourself. Now, what are you getting up to, darling? Are we allowing clients to do oral or not? Oh, we are? Okay, but you know you really shouldn't, don't you, darling? I hope we're always, but *always*, making sure our clients are wearing a condom? Yes? Good girl. Now, let's see what we're going to test you for.'

The nurse ran her pen down the page on her clipboard, ticking a variety of boxes on her long list of sexual diseases, which included everything from HIV to syphilis, and many I'd never heard of. Then she took several tubes of blood from me, putting them all in a kidney dish along with the list. The results, she told me, sticking a plaster on my arm, would be back in a few days' time.

I dashed back into the clinic a few days later, once again on the way to collect the children from school. My mind was very much on other things: it was Thursday, and that meant swimming after school for several of the kids. The car was loaded with towels and costumes, as well as lots of snacks to eat in the car on the way home – they always emerged from swimming absolutely starving. So the bad news from the nurse came as a shock.

'You've tested positive for chlamydia, darling,' the nurse told me.

'Chlamydia?' I asked. I'd never heard of it. What was it, what did it mean?

'It's a fairly common sexual disease that doesn't have any symptoms, but can make you infertile, love,' she told me.

Lucky I've had my babies, I thought. Nevertheless, I wasn't thrilled.

'But can you pass it on?' I asked, alarmed.

'Oh yes. It's quite infectious, darling, and you can easily pass it on through unprotected sex.'

'But I've been so careful,' I said, dismayed, my mind splintering in several directions at once. How had I caught it when I'd always used a condom?

The nurse shrugged gently. She didn't have the answers. She just knew from experience that however careful I was, in the line of work I was in I was always at risk of catching a variety of sexual diseases. This time it was chlamydia. On the scale of possibilities, chlamydia was good news.

The nurse gave me some antibiotics and said she hoped that should deal with it. We agreed I'd come back in three months for another check-up.

'Or sooner if something happens,' she added. 'We're always here to help.'

'Something happens?' I asked, eyes widening.

'Like a condom splits or something, darling,' she explained.

'Oh. Yes.' I nodded in sudden understanding, hoping against hope that would never happen. Please not to me.

I thanked her, and, armed with a bagful of free condoms that she had pressed on me, I went back to the car and sat behind the wheel, silent for a moment. If I had caught chlamydia, despite my precautions, that meant I could catch anything. I popped out an antibiotic from the foil pack and swallowed it as I turned this thought over in my mind. However careful I was, I was clearly at risk: of becoming HIV positive, of getting syphilis. Even of becoming pregnant.

It was a horrible thought and I didn't want to dwell on it. I had no choice. I knew I had to carry on working. I made a mental note never to miss my three-monthly check-up, and in between, I could only pray that none of those things would happen to me. I rammed the bag of condoms deep into my handbag and put the key in the ignition. It was time to go and pick up my children.

By now, Christmas was fast approaching and the days were a whirl of end-of-term plays and carol concerts. One of the only good things about my work, aside from the money, was that I could now attend all these events, which are such important markers in a childhood. In my previous life as a secretary, I'd inevitably missed many of them, since so many took place in the day. Now I was available, if exhausted, to sit in the school hall for any number of events, watching my various children dance, sing or act their way across the stage.

I was beginning to feel quite excited about the approach of Christmas and the fun we'd have as a family. Unlike previous ones, when I'd forced myself to shut my mind to the mounting debts as I shopped for the inevitable trolleyload of presents and food, this time I knew we could afford a little good cheer. And after working hard nearly every night for the whole of the autumn, I felt I deserved a few days off to enjoy life with my children.

Christmas that year was better than we could have anticipated. I just relished my time with the children and the obvious enjoyment in life that they were radiating. They were clearly happy and secure.

I had ensured that happiness for them, I reflected.

Over those few Christmas days, I stored up images of their happy faces smiling round the lunch table, opening their stockings from Santa, in the hope that they would see me through the bleak patches to come in the next few months. I would need the memories to help me through the inevitable low moments that I now knew occurred at two or three in the morning, with three clients behind me and Ant driving me towards an unknown fourth. When I was longing to be safely at home with my kids, tucked up in my own bed asleep, I would bring them up like pictures on a screen to help keep up my motivation. They would remind me that it was all worth it – the tiredness, the outfits, the faked passion, the forced intimacy with strangers. All worth it because it was safeguarding my children's happy lives.

One of the best presents my work bought that Christmas was for Emily – the school choir singing trip to Paris in January. Emily, my eldest child, so responsible, had said nothing to me about it because she had picked up some time before that we had money worries, and, sensitive and thoughtful as she was, didn't want to make the situation any worse with an extra demand. But now, with the money I'd earned, she could go. She deserved it, I told her, because she'd done so well in her Eleven Plus. Her smile nearly split her face.

That was a memory to hang on to during those two-in-the-morning blues.

Chapter Eight

The New Year came and I reluctantly returned to work. From an objective point of view, there was nothing particularly nerveracking about it any more; in a professional sense I was in my stride. I'd been working long enough now to have come to terms with what I was doing, and to have a coping mechanism that enabled me to do it. I knew that what I was doing night after night was simply a job. Somehow I kept it quite separate in my mind from the act of making love with someone I cared for. The two were simply not related.

This was so clear in my mind that I didn't regard myself as being unfaithful to Paul. I had no guilt about him when I went to work every night. It was on the rare occasions that I went to visit David that I felt weighed down with guilt. Even if we didn't do anything, I knew in my heart that I was being unfaithful.

While I was reconciled to the practicalities of my work,

emotionally, as always, I struggled. Going back to work the first night after a wonderful holiday with my kids, from a life far removed from the seedy world of prostitution, wasn't easy. But I dangled a number of carrots in front of myself for motivation, and off I went.

I might be reluctant, but work was going well. My list of regulars was growing and I was quickly finding out that once a client took up with me, they didn't see the need to stop. The ever-growing number of repeat bookings gave my regularly flagging confidence a huge boost – it was like getting a good report at school. It also made my working life easier in practical terms. I now had several weekly bookings with regulars, which gave a good shape to my week. Then, of course, there was a seemingly endless supply of one-off clients, and those, like Rory, who booked me regularly but not frequently because they lived too far away. Thanks to Rory, I'd soon seen every musical playing in London and eaten in all the well-known eateries, from Pont de la Tour to the Ivy.

Some of my regulars were single men just looking for fun, but I'd realised by now that, as I'd initially suspected, there was a large group of nice, normal men who, for one reason or another, were simply incredibly lonely. And it wasn't just single men who were lonely. Their loneliness I could understand – it can be difficult to meet someone if you work long hours all week, particularly if you live in London where no one looks at each other, let alone initiates a conversation. But many of the lonely men I met were married. There seemed to be any number of husbands who were apparently married to nice-looking women, judging by the photos in the hall; yet they were the loneliest of the lot.

This type of client often had me shaking my head in disbelief. More often than not, I'd turn up at a smart house to find a polite, not unattractive man waiting for me. He'd take my coat, offer me a drink, and tell me a little about himself as we sat in his tastefully decorated sitting room, surrounded by all his happy family photographs.

As we chatted over drinks, it would take only the slightest prod for these men to pour forth the detail of their lives. I never forgot during my hours with a client that I was there for their pleasure, whether it was sexual or emotional, so when they told me about their businesses, I would listen with apparent interest and try and ask relevant questions. A little bit of attention, and soon these men would be telling me all about how lonely they were, and how their wives simply weren't interested in them. I lost count of the number of times I heard men tell me that their wives had just 'gone off' sex. 'She says she doesn't like it any more,' they'd say as we climbed the stairs to the bedroom. 'We haven't slept together for ages.'

From where I was in terms of sex, I found this behaviour on the part of the wives absolutely impossible to understand. These women had landed on their feet, so why, with their neglect, were they now taking such colossal risks with their marriages? More often than not, two smart cars sat in the drive, the home was lovely, the school fees were obviously being paid, and no doubt the wife had at least one credit card that worked, yet still they couldn't bring themselves to have sex with the poor man who provided all this? I wasn't expecting them to have marathon sessions on a daily basis, but was a quickie, once or twice a week, really so much to ask?

Apparently it was. I felt rather sorry for husbands like these, and in such circumstances it was hardly surprising that when I turned up, elegantly dressed, expressing interest in the detail of their lives, and ready to give blow jobs and hand jobs on demand, they blossomed like flowers in springtime and promptly booked me again and again. Everyone needs attention in life – and I don't just mean sexual attention.

I didn't flatter myself. I knew from the start that it wasn't me that they enjoyed being with so much; it was the attention I gave them, and that could have come from another woman just as well. It should have come from their wives, and so easily could have – a home-cooked meal now and then, ten minutes' worth of feigned interest in their husbands' work, a blow job once a week – but it didn't. So they'd looked elsewhere, to a call girl – in this instance, me. In a way, their wives were fortunate in that. After all, their husbands could have started having an affair instead, and ended up leaving them. (To be honest, a husband does sometimes leave his wife for a call girl.) Didn't these wives realise that, by neglecting their husbands, they risked losing everything? There were times when I almost wanted to leave them a note. 'Alert: your husband is having sex with a call girl on a regular basis. Give him a bit of attention before it's too late!'

Of course I didn't. And at least husbands like this were safe with me. I was never a threat to the marriage. I was in it for the money and nothing else. No strings attached either way. But still, by seeing me, a husband had taken a step down a road that might, eventually, lead him away from his marriage.

However, there was a limit to how much I could worry for these wives. I knew as I closed the door after each booking that, ultimately, whether the husband eventually left or not was the wife's problem. I was just the call girl.

Some clients were so lonely that they'd book me for several nights a week, every week, until something happened to break the cycle. This something might be their money running out, as at £150 an hour an addiction to me wasn't a cheap habit to sustain, or they might find a girlfriend.

Steve was an accountant, who lived in London. I first visited him early in the New Year. He opened the door to me and invited me in as if I was an old friend.

'Come in, sit down, have a drink,' he said, taking me through to the sitting room.

He'd been watching the television, some kind of detective programme I noticed, and it was still on. I sat on the sofa next to him, clutching my drink, and he began to fill me in on what had happened so far in the programme. 'So you'll understand what's happening,' he said, as if I was here to watch television.

There were several empty beer cans on the coffee table in front of us. He looked nice enough – medium height, untidy dark hair and a five-o'clock shadow – but perhaps he was a big drinker?

'Shall we go upstairs?' I suggested.

'Why don't we just talk first, watch a bit of telly, relax,' he countered.

He was paying by the hour, so that was fine by me. I sat back, and with half an eye on the television we began to talk. It was like a cork popping out of a bottle. Steve told me about the pressures of his job, and how lonely he was in his personal life. All his old friends were married with kids, and he didn't have the energy at night to go out and meet new people.

'So I use your agency,' he concluded, as if it was a dating agency rather than one providing girls for sex. It was clearly company he was mostly after; the sex was almost an afterthought. We did have sex – the usual routine: massage on both sides followed by a blow job and me leaping about on top of him – but it was just a small part of the evening, rather than its focus.

That set the pattern for many evenings to come, and for me it was an easy and pleasant enough booking during what were often very busy nights. Five or so nights a week, I'd go to Steve for two hours. He might get a takeaway, or cook something, and we'd chat – a lot – before having sex.

Poor man. He was successful, well off and single, and his way of coping with his loneliness was to drink beer and book me. I was really glad for him when, after about seven months, he told me he'd met a girl.

'I want to give it a chance with her,' he said, rather apologetically, almost as if he was dumping me.

I told him he didn't need to feel guilty, or worry about me. I said I was thrilled for him, and really hoped it worked out. Apart from the practical fact that I'd lost a good client, I genuinely meant it. Anyway, I knew there was plenty more work out there. I wanted the best for him, and I knew that didn't mean booking me five nights a week.

I didn't hear from him again, and I'm hoping that the girl he met is the reason why. Sometimes I picture him, married to her by now, with a couple of kids. I hope I'm right, and that life worked out for him.

There was no shortage of replacements when a client like Steve left. Another weekly regular who took up with me about this time was a married man, but his was quite a different kind of marriage from most of the others. It was a very tragic story.

I got a call to go to a client called Peter. Peter showed me into his sitting room, which was full of photos of him with his arms round a beautiful blonde woman. They looked so happy in the photos, I couldn't quite believe that this was yet another husband whose wife didn't want to sleep with him. Peter must have noticed my gaze.

'Let me explain.' He coughed, clearly embarrassed. 'It's not what it seems. I love her so much. But – she's ill, you see. She had a heart attack seven months ago, and her brain was starved of oxygen. She's in hospital. I visit every day.'

'How absolutely dreadful for you both. You don't have to explain it to me,' I assured him, feeling so sorry for him in all his embarrassment and misery. But he went on regardless, as if he really needed to feel I understood.

'I just feel terribly, terribly guilty about it, but I'm desperate for some sex.'

'Of course you are,' I soothed. 'It doesn't mean you don't love your wife. You're just a normal man with a sex drive.'

Peter fell on my words gratefully. 'Oh, do you think so? I love her so much, I've never been unfaithful before, it's just been so long . . .' He tailed off.

'I know, you poor thing,' I said. 'Shall we start with a massage?'

Peter led the way upstairs.

The roll-call of the lonely was endless. There was Tom, a marketing consultant, who was clinically obese. He had earned a great deal of money working abroad, and had returned to England, the place of his childhood, hoping that he might meet a nice girl to settle down with. But his size put everyone off. In desperation, he rang the agency and ended up with me. I didn't really mind if they were fat or thin, old or young, so long as they were clean, treated me like a human being, and, of course, paid. So when Tom opened the door to me, I wasn't horrified. By now I was used to all sorts, and nothing fazed me.

The first night I went to Tom's house was a warm summer's evening. He led me through the house to where he had a hot tub in his garden. We both stripped off and sat in the tub, which was bubbling away, drinks in hand. I sidled up to him and began to stroke the leg that was closest to me, and he looked at me so gratefully it was clear he had very little physical contact with human beings.

After that, Tom booked me almost every night. Given his size, it was very hard to have sex with Tom. Hand jobs and blow jobs were easier. Sometimes, he didn't want sex at all and we just chatted. And every time I visited, night after night, he had always bought me a little gift – a bottle of wine or some chocolates. He was a vast man with an even larger heart. It was just a shame that he looked the way he did.

Joseph, an engineer who lived in South London, was so lonely he quickly decided he was in love with me. I visited him once every fortnight or so. He was gentle and thoughtful, and since he didn't earn that much and I was expensive, I'd always try to get to his booking early and spend a little more time with him than he had paid for.

But this kindness eventually backfired.

'Marry me,' Joseph pleaded towards the end of our second year of visits. 'You could stop work, stay at home. I'll put your son through public school, I earn enough.'

'It's a nice offer, Joseph, but I'm afraid the answer's no,' I said, trying to let him down as gently as possible.

'But I love you, Elizabeth,' he cried.

You don't even know my real name, I thought sadly, letting myself out of his apartment for what I knew was the last time. It was an irony not lost on me that the only man who had ever offered to look after me in all my life was a man who paid me for sex.

I didn't want to turn away business, but I had to tell Trish I couldn't visit Joseph any more. I also began to really encourage Tom and others like him to get out into the world, to try and meet someone. Otherwise, I could foresee that their money would run out and they'd be on their own again. I didn't want that to happen, not just for them, but because it would put me in a difficult position. After all, much as I liked Tom and other clients like him, the reality was that I was spending my time with them for just one reason: money. They might forget that, but I never did. There simply wasn't room for misunderstandings.

Lack of sleep was starting to take its toll on me. Increasingly I was struggling in the mornings. I found it really hard to prise my eyelids apart after three hours' sleep, although Jack and Victoria bouncing on me always helped.

It seemed like I'd been tired for ever. I didn't think it was possible to feel more exhausted than I did. Every morning, as I made the lunch boxes and laid out breakfast, I drank a couple of cups of strong coffee to get me going. Usually this worked. I'd crawl back to bed for a few hours during the day, and somehow that would be enough to get me through. Then, almost overnight, there came a time when even that didn't seem to help. I felt as if I was keeling over with exhaustion.

It must be accumulated tiredness, I thought. I had been working really hard, six nights a week, and repeated short nights weren't made better just by a nap in the day. I gave myself a night off, and slept for twelve hours straight. Usually that gave me a boost in energy terms – I'm the type that bounces back quickly – but this time it made little difference; I woke up shattered. A small, dreadful thought nudged forward in my mind, but I pushed it resolutely away. It simply couldn't be true.

But two mornings later, I knew that it was. Making the

children's egg sandwiches for their lunch boxes, I was suddenly assaulted by a wave of nausea. My heart dropped to the floor. I simply couldn't stand it, I thought, knowing at the same time that I had to. I didn't know how it had happened, or when, but I felt absolutely certain about one thing. I was pregnant.

After dropping the children at school that morning, I went to the chemist and bought a test. I took it home again. My worst fears were confirmed.

I sat at the kitchen table at home, a place that was fast becoming the scene of all my lowest, most despairing moments. Although I had barely had time to take in the news, I knew instinctively that I couldn't have the baby. To start with, I had no idea who the father was. It could be Paul's – occasionally we still had sex – but it could be David's, or, most likely of all, a client's. That meant any one of the forty men I had had sex with in the last three weeks.

How had it happened? I asked myself wearily. Had a condom split, as the nurse at the Dartford health clinic had told me they could? If so, I hadn't been aware of it. But I couldn't think of anything else. I'd been so careful, always using condoms with clients, on top of which, I was also on the pill. Still, something had obviously gone badly wrong.

I knew I had to arrange a termination, and the sooner the better, but I felt ill at the thought. How could this be happening to me? How could I, the loving mother of six wonderful children, the woman who only lived for her children, who was working all hours in a vulnerable, difficult profession for their sake, be arranging to have an abortion? I couldn't help contrasting how I felt about this pregnancy with how I'd always felt before. I was devastated.

A part of me still knows I would have loved to have had that baby, regardless of its uncertain paternity. It has always been easy for me to throw myself into being pregnant and having children. Even now, years later, I still fantasise about having one more child. A little girl, perhaps, called Ruby or Bella. But back then, I knew I couldn't allow myself to even entertain the idea of keeping it. Apart from anything else, it would mean I would have to stop working, and we'd be back at square one. No, I told myself firmly, listing all the other reasons why I couldn't have the baby: my home situation was far from settled; the father was unknown; I was already seriously overcommitted in terms of my time and the number of people I had to love and care for. It was out of the question. I simply couldn't bring this child into the world.

I steeled my heart and mind against the thought of it, and took down a copy of the Yellow Pages. I looked up the number for the nearest Marie Stopes clinic and dialled. I told the woman on the other end of the line the bald truth: that I was pregnant and simply couldn't keep the baby; that I already had six children and was struggling to make ends meet; that another child could tip the balance for all of us. She made understanding noises and I made an appointment for the following day.

That night, I told Paul that I was pregnant. He assumed it was his, of course, but was absolutely horrified at the thought of another child. How far we had come from the days when we would have welcomed a new baby, I thought sadly. But his reaction underlined to me what I already knew: there was just no way I could have it.

I won't go on about the sadness that folded round me like a cloak as the train taking me to the Marie Stopes clinic on the day of the termination drew nearer and nearer to its destination. The staff were nice enough, and had been trained not to judge, but no one could shield me from the misery of what I was doing. The pregnancy was in its early stages, so the termination was carried out under local anaesthetic. I remember the feeling of the tears running down my face and trickling into my ears as I lay on my back while the doctor went about his work. I took a few days off work to recover physically, and at the same time tried to come to terms with what I had done. Despite my misery, I did feel a strange relief as well, that it was over, that it was done.

Those nights at home restored me just a little. Although the circumstances were horrific, staying at home with my children was pure pleasure. To know that I didn't have to rev myself up for a night of sleazy encounters with strangers the moment I'd got the children into bed was a luxury I hadn't had for months. Each night, I lay in a hot bath till the water turned tepid, before crawling between the sheets and reading a little in bed, then falling asleep.

If only things were different. If only every night could be like this, if only I didn't have to work as an escort . . . These thoughts slunk into my mind as I climbed into bed on what I knew was my last night off. I stamped down on them hard. I had to work and that was that. I simply couldn't afford to entertain the notion of not carrying on. I might hate it, but it was saving us all.

Propped up on pillows, the latest John Grisham lying on my lap unopened, I reflected on what I had achieved so far. The building society were now off my case, and the house was no longer under threat. The second repossession hearing had been cancelled by the building society once they had seen how I was making my regular monthly payment as I had promised. It was our largest outgoing, as I was paying not only our regular mortgage payment, but also a large chunk of the arrears that had built up. All the direct debits I'd set up were working well. The bills were no longer thudding on to the doormat with such frightening regularity. Our debts were a long way from being paid off, but I was managing them. So long as I kept earning as I was, our finances were back under control.

But life, I reflected with a sigh, was not cheap. On top of all the direct debits there was day-to-day living to pay for: the supermarket shop every week, and the endless needs of the children. They grew so fast, and I knew it was stupid pride, but I wouldn't let myself buy their uniform from the second-hand shop; everything had to be new. I didn't want anyone looking down on my kids.

When I'd got us out of this mess, I told myself, putting the unopened book on my bedside table and switching off the light, never again would I allow myself to run up such debts; never again would I fail to face up to a bill as it came in. I had learned the hard way that the consequences of that were disastrous – that was the reason why I had to keep on working till goodness knows when, until the debts were gone and I had sufficient savings to think up an alternative way to earn a living. I hoped it wouldn't be too long. I snuggled down under the duvet and closed my eyes. Might as well enjoy my last night of sleep for a while. Tomorrow night it would be work again, and now there was a new worry on my list: how not to get pregnant again. Now that I was aware that it was possible to become pregnant despite the strictest of precautions, it was my chief fear, greater than that of catching some horrible disease, greater than getting beaten up by a client. I knew I couldn't go through the physical and emotional awfulness of a termination again.

About 11 p.m. one evening I came out of a job to find Ant in a lather of excitement.

'I've been listening to the radio, and the DJ is asking anyone listening to ring in and say why they aren't fast asleep in bed by now. What they are doing, still being up at this hour. Well, I thought of you, love. You should ring in and tell them why.'

Sinking back into the seat of the car, I listened to the show for a few minutes. It was the *James Whale Show*.

'So why are you all listening out there? Give me a ring and let me know,' he said.

'Go on,' Ant urged.

Why not, I thought. It would be a laugh.

I rang the number and got through quickly. I told the person vetting calls that I was a call girl and that my name was Elizabeth. That got me through to James in no time at all. I suppose 'call girl' was slightly more unusual than 'night porter' or 'nurse doing shift work'.

'You're Lizzie the hooker,' said the DJ with evident delight.

'Yes,' I admitted, picking up on his light-hearted tone. 'I suppose I am.'

James asked me why I was working as a prostitute, and I told him something of my circumstances although not enough for anyone I knew to recognise me. We chatted a little longer, said goodbye and I rang off.

Ant and I kept on listening in between jobs that night to hear the reaction my story had provoked. It soon became apparent that my call had spurred a lot of people to pick up the phone. Call after call came from listeners with an opinion on my working life, and although James repeatedly tried to provoke a negative reaction, nearly all of them had only a good response to my story. Amazingly, not a single one was saying something along the lines of 'the old slapper should be ashamed of herself'. Instead, there were outpourings of support.

There was Lynn from the Isle of Wight, who wanted Jesus to save me, and any number of cabbies ringing in to say, 'I met her, I saw her struggling along in Knightsbridge,' or, 'I gave her a lift to Hampstead,' or wherever. It seemed like every taxi driver in London knew me . . . Lots more people rang in to say that they heartily approved of what I was doing, and that I was managing marvellously and should be proud of myself. My kids were well looked after while I worked and I wasn't a burden on the taxpayer, which was a great deal more than many other people could claim.

I have to confess that this made me smile. Here I was, doing a job that required huge amounts of lying, that was, in the eyes of society, morally questionable, and yet people from all over the country were giving me a pat on the back for it. Such job recognition was rare in my line of work. After all, prostitution isn't a job with much status. It's not the kind of career that most fathers hope their daughters will adopt. The reaction from the listeners of the *James Whale Show* that night was a rare boost and reminded me that I wasn't doing anything so terrible. Most of the time I just got on with it, earning the money that ensured the stability of my family. Sexual morals are the luxury of the rich.

But although I tried not to, in my lowest, two-o'clock-in-the-morning self-doubting moments, I inevitably questioned what I was doing. Was what I was doing so awful? Had I made the wrong decision? Should I have given up everything we knew and loved and started again? Why hadn't I managed, like so many other women seemed to, to choose a husband who would look after me and my kids? How could I possibly bear to have sex with yet another stranger? What would my children think of me when, one day, they discovered what their mother had done for a living for a while?

Being beset with doubts and a sense of failure was part of the deal, in my experience, so I hung on to the fact that people who didn't know me thought I wasn't so awful – far from it, in fact, just a mother doing right by her kids – and it lifted me considerably. If nothing else, they understood and respected my motivation: that I was doing it for one reason: for my kids.

My first full year of escorting brought about a great change in our finances. Working as hard as I was, I succeeded in sorting out a large part of the backlog of debt, and I was still determinedly staying on top of the costs of our lives and not letting new debts build up. By the time the next Christmas came around, we were in an even better place financially. But having been working nights for well over a year by then, I really was tired.

As I drove away from my home night after night, my heart always lurched, knowing that I wouldn't be back again until four or possibly even five in the morning. Then, hours and hours later, often with dawn breaking around me, I would let myself in and creep up the stairs to bed. I'd get three hours' sleep, if I was lucky, and then I'd be up making lunch boxes, plaiting the girls' hair, making sure everyone had some breakfast before setting off on the school run.

At about 9.30 a.m., I would let myself back in to the now silent house, and, though I was desperate to go to bed, had to tidy away the breakfast first. It was stubborn pride – I wouldn't let standards slip, however tired I was. I couldn't think, Oh, to hell with it, I'll clean it up when I wake up. No, I had to load the dishwasher with six bowls, cups, spoons and juice glasses, wipe the table, put away the cereal boxes, and generally make sure the kitchen was spotless before I'd allow myself the luxury of going back to bed.

After a couple more hours' sleep, I'd get up again. Much as I wanted to sleep all day, there were still so many things to do. First, I had to keep the household running for Paul and the children – washing had to be done and hung out to dry, uniforms ironed, beds changed, costumes made for school plays, and so on and so on. Next, I would turn my attention to the general administration of paying the money I'd earned the night before into the bank, and writing cheques for whichever bills needed paying. Finally, I had to look at myself in terms of the coming night's work. Did my nails need redoing? My eyebrows plucking? Were my outfits clean and ready for use? No sooner had I done this than I'd look at my watch and realise it was time to go and pick up the kids. The cycle of work–home–chores–work was absolutely relentless, and I knew I couldn't carry on at that pace indefinitely.

At the same time, Paul was not enjoying his job. He was complaining each day that his hips hurt. His was a very physical job, which definitely wasn't helping matters, and I began to wonder if there might not be several good reasons for him to give up his job, at least for a while. It would give his body a break, and if he was home during the day he could hopefully take on some of the home responsibilities that I currently had to shoulder. For example, he could get the children up in the morning and take them to school, giving me a chance to catch up properly on my sleep.

I was earning so much money by now that Paul's salary had become a bit of an irrelevance. With so many bills now dealt with, I knew we could manage without it. I also wondered if time out of work would help Paul get his life back on track. He'd always been interested in computers – perhaps he could retrain as a computer programmer or something along those lines, and give himself a whole new take on life to jolt him out of his rut?

As things stood, Paul and I were like ships that passed in the night. I worked while he was at home, and vice versa. I know it sounds strange, unbelievable even, but although I had strong feelings for David, I hadn't quite accepted it was over with Paul. Wouldn't it do us good to spend some time together? And wouldn't it be nice for the kids to see their parents together, for all of us to have time together as a family?

The more I thought about it, the more brilliant an idea it seemed. I felt we'd all benefit from an increase in the quality of life. And with Paul being so uninterested in finances, I didn't think he'd find it so unbelievable that a family of eight could survive well on the salary of one night-working secretary. So one evening I tentatively mentioned it to him.

The idea shocked him at first – he actually took his eyes off the television to look at me when I suggested it. 'What, be a house husband?' he said with some horror. Paul was a very masculine kind of man.

'It wouldn't be like that,' I protested. 'It's just that we can't go on as we are indefinitely. I'm exhausted, and you and I barely see each other. If you gave up work, I could get more sleep and we could spend some time together in the day. And your hips would have time to heal. You could do a course, retrain as a computer consultant, or whatever grabs you. An indoor job might be a better

thing for you. And it needn't be for ever. We could just try it and
see how it worked.'

Paul digested all this.

'Would we be able to manage, moneywise?' he finally asked.
This was the first financial question he had asked for months.

'Yes. Because it's a night shift that no one wants to do, the job's
very well paid, and I've just been given a rise,' I lied glibly. I was
becoming horribly good at lying, much as I hated it.

I continued to outline the benefits in terms of the time it would
give us. Paul seemed quite excited by the idea of retraining. He
said he was willing to get the children up in the morning and take
them to school. This would mean I'd be able to get enough sleep
in one block to carry on with my work for the foreseeable future.
And he admitted that he could see the benefits in financial terms,
and for his health.

'Okay,' I said. 'Why don't you resign tomorrow?'

And he did.

Chapter Nine

*I*t was at about this time that I branched out into a whole new area of escorting. I took a booking with a couple.

When I had first joined the agency, Trish had asked me whether, in principle, I'd be interested in visiting a couple. She told me that lots of girls wouldn't do it, but the moment she told me it paid more, I knew I was going to give it a go. So I said yes, she could consider me if something came up, and promptly forgot all about it.

One night, Ant was waiting for me at Dartford station as usual, with something of a smirk on his face.

'What? What is it?' I wanted to know.

'I've got you a double date, darling,' he grinned.

Although I was totally unprepared – how do you prepare to have sex with a couple? – before I got into a real panic, Ant drew up outside a fairly modest terraced house. The door was opened by a man called Greg. Medium height, grey hair, nothing particularly unusual about him, I thought, as I followed him through to the sitting room.

There, on the sofa, sat his wife, Vanessa, wearing a pale pink baby-doll number with black stockings and suspenders, her dark hair snaking down on to her shoulders.

Oh my God, I thought, stopping in my tracks in the doorway, she looks like Dorian from *Birds of a Feather*.

Vanessa offered me a glass of wine, which I have to say I accepted. It had been a while since I'd needed a boost for my nerves, but suddenly it was as if it was my first job again. I didn't know what to expect. Not only was I about to have sex with two people at once, but I was about to get extremely intimate, for the first time ever, with a woman. I barely had time to worry about this, as Greg, in his enthusiasm, was already ushering us up from our seats.

'Come on,' he said, all matter of fact and clearly keen not to waste any time, 'let's go upstairs.'

In the following hour, I learned why an escort girl is paid more for an appointment with a couple – £200 as opposed to £150. They earn every penny of it.

Up in the bedroom, I stripped down to my black underwear – bra, pretty knickers, suspender belt and stockings. Any assumptions I had made about this sweet little wife and her average husband were dispensed with in moments. Vanessa disappeared for a moment, only to return holding a large double-ended dildo.

Lying on the bed next to Vanessa, I began to fondle her. It felt strange, but not unpleasant, to stroke and kiss her breasts one by one, and to feel her curves. The main thing that struck me was the softness: a woman's body is so much softer than a man's. And although I had never met Vanessa before that night, her body seemed strangely familiar; it was just like my own.

Vanessa responded eagerly to my caresses, and, cottoning on that she liked lots of foreplay – don't most women? – I stroked and kissed her until she said she was ready to use the dildo. Then, as we sat opposite each other, she pushed one end into herself, and the other into me, before switching it on.

Greg, meanwhile, had been standing at the end of the bed, watching. Now, watching us both buzzing away, linked by the dildo, he started wanking as well. Suddenly, he started pissing all over both of us, spraying it around as though his cock was a hose.

Horrified, I looked at Vanessa, to find she was moaning, head back, pert breasts thrust forward, fingering an erect nipple with one hand, clearly loving it all and very probably close to coming. Greg, meanwhile, had followed up his golden shower by spraying us with his semen. I might be utterly revolted, I reflected, but they were obviously having a marvellous time.

The peeing disgusted me, but I didn't allow that to put me off couples in general, or, indeed, Vanessa and Greg, to whom I had several return visits, some of which involved cucumbers, whipped cream, chocolate sauce, syrup, and strap-on dildos. Despite Greg's predilection for 'golden showers', as peeing on people is known in the trade, I even came to quite like them as a couple. They were unusually uncomplicated about it all. Madly in love with each other, they were both extremely sexually adventurous, and were never short of ideas. One evening, their general enthusiasm and excessive bouncing even led to the bed collapsing. But not even this could stop them in their tracks; sprawled on the floor, laughing, Greg carried on fucking Vanessa from behind, while Vanessa carried on fucking me with a strap-on dildo. I think an earthquake or act of God on a similar scale would have been the minimum required to distract them from taking their sexual pleasure.

After my initiation into couples, courtesy of Greg and Vanessa, I took couple bookings willingly. The cold hard facts were, as always, that I was in this to earn the money I needed to shore up my family life. I didn't actively enjoy any of my work, so I might as well try and make each hour that I was effectively performing for another's pleasure pay as well as it could. So sex with couples became part of my ever-expanding repertoire.

I was soon to find out that both parts of a couple weren't always as willing to involve a third party as Greg and Vanessa. I quickly came to realise that, all too often, the man put pressure on the wife or girlfriend to go through with a threesome and she, worried that he'd think her boring or sexually repressed, agreed against her better judgement.

Chris and Susan were a classic example of such a couple: he really wanted a three-in-the-bed sex session, and she couldn't think of anything worse. It was obvious from the moment I met him that Chris was really excited about having two women at once. That didn't surprise me much; after all, it's probably one of most men's top fantasies.

Chris couldn't get me into the house quick enough. He was raring to go. The drawback came when I met his partner, Susan, a few moments later. Chris had told me that she was happy to go through with it, but her body language and facial expression told quite another story. The second I met her it was obvious she was fighting hard to stop herself from crying.

'Are you sure about this, Chris?' I asked, raising my eyebrows in the direction of Susan. I didn't want to talk myself out of a booking, but I'd never seen anyone less eager for sex. Unsurprisingly, I hadn't come across a reluctant client before, and I didn't really know how to deal with it. But Chris impatiently brushed aside my concerns.

'She'll do it,' he said grimly. I disliked him already. I looked at Susan, and she nodded meekly.

So that's the way it is, I thought. He's making her. Probably says he'll leave her if she won't do it. But it wasn't my role to judge or moralise or feel sorry for half of the couple booking me. I was just the call girl, there for their pleasure. As much as I hated it, I had to keep my feelings to myself and get on with the job. I trudged upstairs after them with a sinking heart. I had a feeling this booking might get rather awkward.

Upstairs, all three of us lay on the bed in a state of semi-undress. I had decided on the way up that the best way to handle the situation might be to concentrate on Susan, but it soon became obvious that she couldn't bear me to touch her. Who could blame her? She was probably thinking, God knows where this woman's been. Chris, meanwhile, was all over me, caressing me through my underwear, and then taking it off piece by piece. He seemed to relish undressing me. It was almost as if he was doing it to taunt Susan, who was by now lying next to him, naked, vulnerable and quiet. It gave the whole thing a really unpleasant atmosphere that Chris showed no signs of picking up on. Finally, as he reared up over me and slid himself into me, Susan could stand it no longer and ran from the room sobbing. As I lay there, Chris thrusting himself in and out of me with mounting shouts of pleasure, I could hear her howling from the next room. He clearly didn't care a jot about her misery. He carried on until he came and then rolled off me, lying next to me panting, a satisfied, rather heartless man.

The hour was up. I got dressed, ready to leave. I couldn't go through that again. As I left, I turned to Chris with a little advice.

'If you want to have sex with two girls, I'm happy to see you again, but don't expect Susan to do it. Book another girl from the agency as well as me, and don't tell Susan about it,' I advised.

And that is exactly what he did.

Now that Paul had given up his job, things were a little easier at home. At least I was getting enough sleep to cope with my long nights, and Paul was helping a little with the household chores. He'd do the washing, or the food shopping. The load I was carrying seemed a little lighter.

But in personal terms, Paul wasn't making any headway. Despite the fact that he now had a chunk of every day at his disposal, he didn't show any interest in doing anything constructive with it. The brochures that I requested on his behalf from the local college just lay about the sitting room, unread. It was becoming increasingly clear that his interest in retraining had been fleeting. Now he seemed content for days to drift by with him barely registering their passing.

I became more and more frustrated as the months passed. What was wrong with the man? He was clearly very unhappy but, try as I did, I just couldn't seem to get through to him. Emotionally he'd retreated to a place beyond my reach. It was as if he didn't seem to care about what happened to him or to me or to us. I'd known in my heart for a while that our relationship wasn't working, but what about his children? They needed him, loved him. Couldn't he wake up from his reverie and come back to us, for their sake?

Of course it was the kids I worried about most, particularly the older ones who were by now understanding much of what was going on. But whichever way I turned I couldn't see a solution, apart from the one I dreaded most. Asking Paul to leave. Admitting my marriage was over.

Every time the thought came up, I dismissed it instantly. Surely it hadn't come to that? But more and more frequently now, even as I squashed the voice inside me, another part of me would ask: 'So, what exactly will it take before you call "time" on this marriage?'

The answer was just around the corner. I don't want to go into details of the event: the night that things came to a head was so awful I simply can't relive it, not for me nor for the sake of my children. And perhaps some things are better left unsaid. Suffice it to say that one evening Paul and I disagreed to such a level and in such a way that he left and moved back in with his parents.

The next few days were very strange. Part of me couldn't believe Paul wasn't there every time I came home, yet part of me relished the calm that came hand in hand with his absence. But still, inside me I grieved for the loss of my gentle giant, my kind, lovely Paul, the man I had sailed into married life with, full of such hope. How could those hopes really be so utterly dashed now? How could my husband have changed into someone I no longer recognised? How could my children really be facing life as products of a split home?

Time and again, I forced myself to reconsider. Had I made a mistake? Endlessly, I turned the question over and over in my mind like a pebble in my hand but, dominated by emotions, I simply didn't know.

Paul, however, had already decided that I had. He rang me several times every day, begging to come back, and as the days went by his constant calls and promises began to wear me down. The children did miss him, I reasoned, perhaps we should give it one final chance, after all? Had I been wrong in thinking we had nowhere else to go together? As I wrestled with my feelings, I confided in a close friend, who told me starkly that I was mad to even think about it. But while it was easy for her to be objective, still I couldn't quite accept that Paul was gone for good. I can only conclude from my experience that it is very hard for a person to admit a marriage is truly dead.

The phone calls kept coming, Christmas was approaching, and the little voice in my head kept telling me that I just might have got it all wrong. Shouldn't I give it one last go, to be sure? Paul could come back, play Santa Claus on Christmas Eve, carve the turkey on Christmas Day, hug the kids. He could help Alexander set up the Scalextric set I'd bought him from us; build some amazing Lego with Jack. The more I thought about it, the more I could see it: surely we could be that family?

And so one day in mid-December Paul came home. The children were thrilled to see him but, inevitably, within a couple of days all the problems we faced were even more evident than previously. Before I knew it, Paul settled back into exactly the same pattern of behaviour that he had had before he left for our trial separation.

As things deteriorated, I found myself standing back, almost outside myself, like an unseen visitor in the corner of the sitting room, and watching events unfold. And what I saw was so awful, so depressing, that I knew then it was better for all of us if it ended. I just had to accept it. Resisting it was simply going to subject us all to more dreadful scenes.

And so it was, as those rather terrible days inched by over Christmas, that I forced myself to understand that, for the sake of all of us, Paul had to move out for good. His behaviour had not changed and it was clear it never would. There was no point thinking only of the guilt I felt that my children were going to have separated parents. For now, devastating as it was to admit it, I knew it would be better for them to face that than for Paul and me to continue together as we were. That was how far we had come. For the sake of the children, and for myself, in the interests of maintaining harmony and stability, Paul and I had to be apart.

As clearly as I had seen the fantasy of what we might have been, now I saw the reality. We were no longer even limping along; we had come to a grinding and permanent halt. My family dream had finally, irreversibly, collapsed. Perhaps it had been an unreal ambition all along. Perhaps there simply were no happy-ever-afters. I felt desperately sad, but I knew I did still have my wonderful, talented, mischievous children. I was determined that every other part of their lives should be as stable as possible.

One night soon afterwards, when the children were all in bed, I slowly climbed the stairs to our bedroom, where Paul was lying in bed watching television. He looked at me with a complete lack of interest.

'This has to stop,' I said.

'It will—,' said Paul.

I held up my hand. 'No, Paul. I've heard it too often. I mean, this marriage has to stop. It's over. I can't do it any more. I'm sorry.'

Paul looked at me for a moment, then nodded. He put up no fight. He knew I was right. There was nothing left between us.

I went to the cupboard and pulled out a large suitcase. I began to pack for him, sadness pervading me. As I piled in his trousers and his shirts, his jumpers, his washbag, Paul silently got out of bed and put on his clothes. I zipped up the case, and together we took it downstairs.

'Where will you go?' I asked him as we stood in the hall facing each other.

He shrugged as if he didn't care very much. 'To my mum's,' he said. He seemed almost relieved. Back to where he had come from, before he had moved in with me all those years ago.

'Goodbye, Paul,' I said, permeated to my core with a deep sense of sadness at our failure.

Paul picked up his case and walked out of the house. He didn't look back. I watched him walk down the street, an increasingly small silhouette of a figure in the lamplight, until he turned the corner and was gone.

I shut the door, and leant against it for a second. I exhaled. It felt like I had almost forgotten how to breathe. Suddenly, something struck me. I listened for a moment. There was absolutely no sound: the children were all asleep, the television was switched off. The house was steeped in silence.

I picked up an empty beer can from the coffee table, walked slowly back into the kitchen and threw it in the bin. The remains of the children's tea was on the table. As I mechanically started to load the dishwasher, there was room for only one thought in my head: my marriage was finally over.

Chapter Ten

The children took Paul's departure better than I'd dared to hope. Certainly his leaving didn't come as a total surprise. And perhaps, like me, they'd had enough of the roller coaster of uncertainty that life with Paul meant by now: would it be calm or stormy? It was all too unsettling. Life without him would, at least, be steady and predictable. I reassured them that we would still see Daddy a great deal, at weekends, and perhaps sometimes after school. They accepted all this without question, and we all got on with the business of the start of the spring term.

There were some practical problems that I had to resolve. Now that I was to all intents and purposes a single mother, I was doing absolutely everything myself: school runs in both directions and all the household chores. This was exhausting, but I could manage it. The bigger problem was that I needed someone to babysit the children at night while I was at work. I had to sort this out fast, as

I couldn't afford to take many nights off. I put up cards in the local newsagents, and rang around my friends. I scoured the adverts in the local papers for some suitable-sounding Mary Poppins figure without any luck. The days ticked by.

It wasn't long before the old panic over finances began to rise. The numerous direct debits I'd set up relied on me earning a certain amount each month, and to do that I had to keep going to work, night after night. But now, suddenly, I couldn't. Night after night, I had to ring Trish and tell her I couldn't work, while I frantically tried to come up with a solution. One night, Sarah covered for me, but I couldn't rely on her every night. I needed a regular, responsible babysitter, and if I didn't find one soon, all my carefully laid plans were going to come down like a house of cards.

One evening, two weeks after Paul had left, I was preparing the children's tea, all the while fretting about whether I was going to be able to keep up the monthly payments. I'd only managed to work one night in all the time since Paul had left. As I stirred the baked beans, I thought about the bills the children had brought home with them that afternoon. With the new term just started, four sets of school fees were due. Thanks to the change in my financial approach – an approach which meant fronting up to bills, not stuffing them in the kitchen drawer – I could pay these with the money I'd put by every month in anticipation of this moment. However, that wiped out the savings. If our life was to stay on the rails, I *had* to get back to work. Otherwise, in a matter of weeks, I wouldn't be able to pay the direct debits, the mortgage, for food, or for the car. It was frightening how fast a well-structured financial plan could go down.

As I grilled sausages and turned over the oven chips, I mentally searched my address book yet again for someone who could help me.

Alice bounced in. 'Mummy, my hockey stick broke today, I need a new one by Thursday. I'm playing in the match after school.'

'Okay, darling,' I said, thinking, Great, that's another £40.

Just then, my mobile phone rang. It was Trish with details of a job that night.

'It's a really well-paid one,' she told me. 'And I know this guy. If it goes well, it'll turn into a well-paid regular.'

I chewed my lip. If I took it, it meant leaving Emily – fourteen by now – in charge of everyone, although I knew Sarah would be over here in a flash if Emily needed her. On the other hand, a good job would make up some of what I hadn't managed to earn in the days since Paul had left. I thought of the direct debits, the mortgage, and Alice's new hockey stick.

'It doesn't start until nine-thirty,' Trish wheedled. 'And you'd be home three hours later.' She clearly wanted me to say yes.

At least the late start meant I could settle all the kids before I left, and I wouldn't be that late back.

'All right,' I said reluctantly. It wasn't just the hole in my balance sheet that made me feel I had to take it; I was also frightened Trish would stop offering me jobs if I refused to work yet again. She'd think I wasn't able to do it any more, and that would be a disaster. How else would our ship stay afloat?

I replaced the receiver and turned back to the task of making tea. Emily wandered in.

'Emily, darling, can you set the table? And call everyone through to wash their hands?'

As I served up, my mood felt slightly lighter. I looked around the table at my six well-fed, well-kept children, happily eating sausages and squabbling over the last of the chips. I made this normal family life possible, I reminded myself. That was why I was going out to work tonight.

I left the younger ones settled and asleep, with instructions to Emily to call Sarah immediately if she needed her.

'Or call me. I'll be back as fast as I can if you need me,' I said, kissing my responsible fourteen-year-old goodbye.

'Don't worry, Mum,' she said. 'We'll be fine.'

Nevertheless, I felt unbelievably anxious about leaving them all.

'Come on, Ant,' I said, 'let's make it as quick as we can.' The sooner I was there, the sooner I would be home again. Nerves gnawed at my gut. Was I making a terrible decision?

As it turned out, I was. Halfway through the job, I nipped into the bathroom to check my phone for messages, and found a message from Sarah. It seemed that someone had called the police and told them my children were home alone.

Fear surged through me. I didn't need the police involved in my life. I made my excuses to the client as I stumbled back into my clothes, and rushed downstairs to Ant.

'Take me home, please, quick,' I begged. As Ant set off, I rang Sarah back on her mobile.

'Don't panic,' she told me. 'I've dealt with the police.' Apparently they had been called out by a nosy neighbour, who had seen me drive off with Ant – it was one of the rare times he had picked me up from home. 'But I don't think it's a good idea for you to do it again,' she added.

I completely agreed. I'd thought the legal babysitting age was fourteen, but it wasn't. I'd made the wrong decision, albeit for good reasons. Now I had to face the cold hard facts: I had to get my babysitting properly sorted out or I couldn't go back to work.

Luckily, a friend came to the rescue the very next day. Her daughter, Hattie, whom I had known since the age of two, was now seventeen and studying for A levels. She was, I knew, responsible and kind. She also wanted to earn some money. Her mother had seen my advert in the newsagent's window, and rang to suggest that perhaps her daughter and a couple of her friends would be interested in setting up a rota, taking two nights each a week to stay over at my house. I would pay them something, and in return they would settle the children and still have time to study for their exams. Since I got back so late, they'd stay the night on the sofa bed in the playroom and leave from my house for their school the next day.

I met Hattie's two friends, and we agreed to a trial period.

From the start it worked better than I had dared to hope. Within days I found myself having far more peace of mind while I was at work than I had thought I would. All the children, for their part, also seemed happier. They liked their babysitters, who were able to do many things that Paul wouldn't always do, like helping them to wash their hair, or helping with their homework. My household quickly settled down into a happy rhythm. It was frightening how fast we closed over the hole that should have been left gaping after Paul's departure, but there was no sense of an empty chair at the kitchen table, no feeling of a member of the family being absent. It was almost as if Paul had never been there.

I still stored my bag of tricks at Sarah's, as I didn't want to run the risk of the children finding Mummy's dressing-up clothes. After more than two years in the business, it was bulging by now. It contained things that I wouldn't have had the first idea what to do with at the outset of my days as a working girl. Some of the stuff I'd bought for general use, but there were also some bits and pieces that I'd started to buy to order at the request of a few regular clients. If a client wanted me to dress in something particular or to bring a certain piece of equipment, but couldn't buy and store it themselves for some good reason (perhaps a wife might find it and wonder what the hell her husband was up to), they'd pay me up front, and I'd go and buy it before our next encounter.

Brian was one of those who wanted something a little unusual. He was six foot tall, blond and athletic, and I visited him twice in the space of ten days, when we went through the usual routine of massage and sex. He had just settled up with me after the second session when he finally summoned up the courage to mention what he'd really like.

I was tucking the money into my purse and preparing to leave when he caught my elbow.

'Elizabeth. I was wondering – how do you feel about domination?' he asked, with just a trace of embarrassment.

'Well, I'm quite happy with me doing it to you, but not the other way round,' I said. Honestly, the things I could discuss frankly without blushing these days.

Brian beamed at me. This obviously fitted in with his plans perfectly.

'Okay,' he said. 'If I get a few things together, would you come round and play one night next week?'

'Absolutely,' I said. 'Ring the agency and fix a time.'

Brian fished another £50 note out of his pocket. 'Get something nice to wear,' he said. By nice he meant 'suitable for a domination game'. I knew then that he was in earnest.

One afternoon a few days later, the agency rang me and told me I had a booking with Brian for the whole evening. I caught the train to Dartford wearing my long burgundy winter coat buttoned up to its rounded collar. As I looked about the train at the collection of tired commuters on their way home, suits rumpled, make-up smudged, it amused me to think that they had absolutely no idea what I was wearing underneath my demure-looking coat: a short black PVC dress with a corset-style top, fishnet stockings and very high-heeled black shoes. By my side was my case, containing a schoolmaster's cane and a paddle, amongst other things.

Ant picked me up from Dartford as usual, and dropped me at Brian's. He was going to wait for me and take me home when I'd finished. While I was waiting for Brian to open the door, I took off my coat and revealed myself in all my dominatrix glory. That way the game would begin from the outset, which I felt instinctively was what Brian wanted.

It seemed I was right. Brian opened the door stark naked.

'Hello, Elizabeth,' he said.

'How dare you call me Elizabeth?' I asked sternly, walking into the house. I put down my coat and opened my case, from which I took the cane and the paddle. Then I turned to Brian.

'You are to address me as Mistress,' I said severely.

'Yes, Mistress,' Brian said meekly.

'And you are not to look at me unless I tell you to. Is that clear?'

'Yes, Mistress.' Brian dropped his head.

'Good. Now,' I said, taking a quick look around the room. I noticed Brian had put out a bench, next to which sat a collection of handcuffs, ties and gags, whips, canes, a cat-o'-nine tails and a very small vibrator. He's really gone to town, I thought. 'Sit in that chair.'

Brian sat. He was already hard.

'Put your hands out in front of you,' I commanded.

Brian did so, and I promptly handcuffed them. I tied his legs to the chair legs and began to circle him slowly.

'You are my slave and you must do my bidding. Is that clear?'

'Yes,' he whispered.

'Yes what?' I bellowed. I felt faintly ridiculous, and was making it up as I went along, but from Brian's reaction it was obviously working.

'Yes, Mistress,' he said.

'That's better.'

After a bit more of this, I stopped in front of him and started wanking him off. He came in about twenty seconds. I left him for a few minutes to recover, then went on with the game.

'Oh dear, oh dear. You enjoyed that, didn't you?'

'Yes, Mistress.'

'Well, you know what that means, don't you?'

'No, Mistress.'

'It means a punishment.'

'Yes, Mistress.'

'It means a whipping,' I said, untying him.

'Yes, Mistress.' I could hear the excitement building in his voice. His cock was already starting to harden again.

'Bend over that bench,' I instructed.

'Yes, Mistress,' he said, eagerly doing as I'd asked, and sticking his arse up in the air.

I began to whip him with the cane I had brought. I began quite gently; I didn't want to hit him too hard. I know it sounds ridiculous, since that was obviously the point, but I was frightened of hurting him. Brian, however, was clearly loving it and begging me to whip him harder.

'Oh, harder, Mistress. I deserve it. Harder.'

So I began swishing the cane a little harder towards his arse.

'Oh, Mistress,' he groaned.

After a while, I stopped and told him he could sit up.

'Thank you, Mistress,' he mumbled.

'Sit there. Watch me,' I said. I began to play with myself with a vibrator I had brought. 'You can watch, but you can't touch,' I instructed.

Brian was clearly longing to touch me, but, forbidden, he began to play with himself instead.

'Stop that at once,' I commanded. 'Did I say you could do that?'

'No, Mistress.'

'Precisely. For that you will have to be whipped again. Lie on the floor and put your bottom in the air.'

Brian did as I asked. I stood over him for a moment, letting him anticipate what was coming.

'You know I am going to beat you, don't you?'

'Yes, Mistress.' Brian's voice throbbed with excitement.

'I will give you a choice. How shall I beat you? One stroke with the cane or three with the paddle?'

'Three with the paddle, Mistress,' he gasped.

I picked up the paddle.

'Right. I shall beat you now, Brian. There is nothing you can do about it. You have to take your punishment.'

Brian could hardly wait. As the paddle connected with his arse on the second stroke, he came again.

I reflected on the well-worn phrase, 'one man's pleasure is another man's pain'. I couldn't think of anything worse than letting a client beat me, but Brian simply couldn't have been enjoying himself more than he was. I allowed him five minutes to recover, then I blindfolded him and told him to bend over the bench.

'No one told you to come,' I said sternly. 'You have a whipping coming to you for that.'

This time I used the cane, and as he begged me to whip him harder, I did, swishing the cane through the air with increasing ferocity. Weals began to rise on his arse, but still he begged for more. How much whipping could a man take? I wondered. Seemingly a great deal.

Eager to keep some variety in the evening, I stopped whipping him after a while, and, with him still bent over the bench, stroked him, fondling his balls and his cock, which was hard as rock once again. I picked up his vibrator and slowly inserted it into his arse-hole. Then I slid my hands between his legs and played with his cock. Soon, Brian came again.

'Oh dear, oh dear,' I mocked. 'You're going to have to be beaten really hard for that, aren't you? And after you've been beaten, I'm going to tie you up on the bed and fuck you.'

'Yes, Mistress,' sighed Brian, in sheer, undiluted ecstasy.

Although clients like Brian were in the minority, he wasn't the only one who liked to be whipped and ordered about. I came to realise that it was often a certain type of man that was into domination. Some high-powered men who had important jobs where they had to make decisions all day long liked nothing better than being told what to do when it came to sex, particularly when accompanied by a large dose of corporal punishment. I pushed aside quizzical thoughts about what kind of overbearing mothers these guys must surely have had, and instead simply aimed to please. After all, the kinkier the sex, the better the pay. Guys into domination generally booked me for longer and tipped well at the end of the night, so I tried not to think about how silly I must look, parading about in my scanty get-up and dishing out orders like a drill sergeant.

While work carried on being as colourful and varied as ever, life at home without Paul opened up a new opportunity for me. Now I was a single woman again, I no longer felt guilty about seeing David.

Nor did we have to skulk about in an illicit manner any more, because David was also single by now. He had left his long-term partner some time ago, and moved to a house of his own just five minutes from us. Occasionally, while Paul and I were still technically together, I'd managed to slip off to David's house for a few snatched, joyous hours; but on those illicit outings guilt had always been my silent disapproving companion. Now I was free in every sense to spend time openly with him.

It was a swift and welcome change. Overnight, we had gone from being unable to walk down the street together to David coming over and meeting the children. He started to spend much of every weekend with us, and while he wasn't particularly demonstrative to the children, I knew that in his own quiet way he liked them.

He also proved himself early on to be very good in a crisis. One night, on a weekend soon after Paul had left, Jack, who was four by now, started to have problems breathing. He'd had a cough for a couple of days, as kids his age often do during the winter months, but that night, as he tossed around in his little bed, unable to settle to sleep, I noticed that he had started to wheeze. Feeling slightly panicked, I called David in – after all, he had two children of his own – and asked him what he thought. He sat on the side of Jack's bed for a moment, watching his chest go up and down.

'He's working really hard to breathe,' he said. 'I think we should get him checked.'

David had confirmed my own thoughts. I quickly got Jack into his dressing gown, while David rang a friend who lived nearby to come and babysit. He arrived within minutes, and with a blanket wrapped around Jack, David scooped him up and carried him to the car. I sat in the back seat cradling Jack as he wheezed away, while David drove us to the hospital. I couldn't get there quickly enough.

Once there, David helped us in, and since children were given priority, soon we were seeing a nurse.

'He's having an asthma attack,' she quickly diagnosed, putting a mask over his face and instructing Jack to breathe in and out as deeply as he could. 'This will make those nasty wheezes better, dear,' she said to him. It was like magic. Within minutes I could see Jack starting to relax, to look around him, no longer focusing all his energy on breathing. I exhaled myself for what felt like the first time in hours, tears pricking the back of my eyes. I blinked them away, holding Jack tight on my lap. Thank God. He was going to be all right.

David stroked my back. 'He's going to be fine,' he said firmly. It was such a novel experience for me to have a solid partner helping me in a crisis. I'd had so many years of Paul simply not getting involved, years of coping with everything myself. I smiled up at him gratefully.

'Thank you so much, David,' I said.

'You ought to let Paul know,' he advised. 'If it was me I'd want to know.'

Silently we both thought of David's boys for a moment, now living with their mother Laura. I knew he was right. I left Jack with David and the nurse for a moment, and went out to use my mobile. I punched in Paul's number, but the phone just rang and rang.

I went back inside. 'He's not answering,' I said. 'He must be out.'

David thought for a moment. 'Why don't you write him a note and I'll go and put it through his door?'

So I did as David suggested.

Much later, back home again with Jack asleep in bed once more, breathing normally, and armed with an inhaler and a series of instructions about what to do if it happened again, I cuddled up against David's warm, sleeping form. Finally, I thought, as I drifted off to sleep, finally, this time I've really done it. I've really, really met my Mr Right.

Ridiculous, I know. I was thirtysomething years old, mother of six children, with two failed marriages behind me and a full-time career as a prostitute – and I still believed in fairy tales. I still believed in knights on white chargers sweeping damsels off their feet and carrying them into the happy-ever-after.

*

223

So there I was, sliding ever deeper in love with David. I loved having him around, sharing so much of my life. We did things together as a family, often with his children as well, making up a great big gang of kids. One Sunday we all went kayaking on a nearby lake, with David helping all the kids get the hang of it. During the week he'd pop round to see me and end up helping the children with their homework. Although I tried not to, I couldn't help comparing Paul unfavourably with him.

But as my personal happiness grew, there was a dark shadow that grew accordingly, and, although I longed to, I couldn't deny its existence. Whenever I thought about it, my stomach curled up in anxiety. Now that I saw David so often, I was lying to him more and more – every day now. He was interested in my work, and asked me quite a lot of questions about it. He seemed to find it quite remarkable that I could earn enough, even working as a night secretary, to cover our conspicuously high standard of living.

'How do you manage?' he'd asked me more than once already. 'Five sets of school fees, a mortgage on a nice house, and all the weekly bills to keep up with. You must be some secretary.'

'Paul gives me a bit,' I lied. Oh God, more lies. 'And yes, I'm good at my job,' I said, before hastily changing the subject.

I tried hard to keep off the subject of my work. Since David remembered every detail about my invented work colleagues I was terrified I'd slip up and he'd find out not only that I was a liar but that I was a call girl. Admittedly with the best motives, but still.

Occasionally, I allowed myself to ask those dark, dangerous questions that I felt sure would come with answers I wouldn't be able to cope with. If David found me out, what would he think of me? Would he hate me, for the lies I'd told, and for what I did for a living? Very probably, I thought in despair. And even leaving aside the lies I'd told him for a moment, how many boyfriends could cope with a girlfriend on the game? If I had to hazard a guess, not many. If David found out what I was up to, wouldn't he just think of all the men I'd slept with and run a mile? Wouldn't that be the last I'd ever see of him? I'd just spend the rest of my life knowing he was out there somewhere, hating me.

That was the most terrifying thought of all – that now, just as I'd found him, I might lose him and his love for me. I could hardly bear to think about it. So most of the time I didn't. I kept my head firmly in the sand and lived in the happy, love-filled moment.

The combination of my work and my children meant it was easy not to think about the threat of David finding me out. My life was so very busy that too often my thoughts were running to catch up with me. As any mother knows, life with children takes on a momentum all of its own. Certainly they had a social life that far outstripped mine. There were always birthday parties to go to or sleepovers to arrange, matches to cheer them on in and plays to watch. And school, where they spent so many of their waking hours, was a busy, thriving place that, like all good schools, required a significant amount of parental input.

I didn't automatically click with most of the other mothers; they reminded me too much of my own mother, the way they looked you up and down as you approached before mentally allocating you a box. However, I knew that my kids wanted me to be a part of their world, and so I had thrown myself in the deep end from the start.

Luckily one mother I really liked was Debbie, who ran the Parent-Teacher Association. Down to earth, the mother of four boys, one of whom was Victoria's best friend, Debbie ran the PTA with an easy, organised hand. I always turned up to the meetings because I wanted to know what was going on in school life. Yet sometimes, inevitably, the demands of school clashed with my other life.

One Wednesday evening at the start of the summer term, we were all crowded into the school hall, sipping lukewarm white wine while Debbie outlined the main agenda of the night: the planning of the summer fair. As usual, I was to be in charge of running the cake stall. I'd arranged for Ant to pick me up outside the school at 8.30 p.m. This should have given plenty of time for the meeting, but unfortunately we'd got off to a slower start than I'd expected. One of the tweed and pearls mothers had scratched her new 4×4 on the way there and had wept trails of midnight blue mascara down both cheeks at the thought of telling her banker husband. She'd needed a lot of calming down from the other mothers before the meeting could properly begin. Now, with the meeting barely under way, it was already 8.15 p.m.

I took out my phone and sent Ant a text. 'Running late. Text when we have booking.' Hopefully that would buy me a little more time. We'd already done the tombola and the raffle. Hopefully Debbie would reach the cake stall any minute.

I kept glancing nervously at my watch as the intricate workings of a secondhand bookstall, a lucky dip, and a hot-dog stand all came up for discussion. I jiggled my foot impatiently. Was this really necessary? The fair was the same every single year. Nothing had changed. Why on earth did the meeting have to go on so long?

'Which brings me on to cakes,' Debbie said. Finally! I was on! I exhaled with relief.

Debbie continued. 'This is, as usual, in the capable hands of—'

Just then my mobile beeped. It was a message from Ant. 'First job in.'

'Now over to you, dear.' Debbie gestured in my direction.

'Just that all cake donations are welcome as usual. And perhaps we could have a section that are nut-free, so the children with nut allergies can buy them in confidence?' I gabbled.

'Now what a good idea that is,' Debbie exclaimed. From the nods I could tell the other mothers thought so too. Great, hopefully I'd made my mark and could nip out in a minute or so. But just then, a hand shot up. 'We could extend that to a wheat-free, dairy-free, egg-free range,' began one mother. I cursed under my breath. Oh, stupid, stupid me. What had I gone and started? My mobile beeped. Ant again.

I texted back: '2 mins.'

'I have a fantastic fat-free recipe for blueberry muffins,' another voice piped up.

I crossed and uncrossed my legs. I knew I had to go.

Suddenly I noticed that the hall had fallen silent. All the mothers were looking at me, waiting for a response.

'All great ideas, ladies,' I said. 'Let's firm them up nearer the time. I'm so sorry, but I've just had a text from the babysitter. One of my children isn't well, and I have to go. But just to reiterate, I'm delighted to be running the stall again, and all contributions will, of course, be very welcome.'

With that, I smiled at everyone and practically ran out of the hall.

Outside the school gates, Ant was waiting, engine running.

'Where are we off to, Ant?' I asked, climbing in.

'A client in South London,' Ant replied.

He pulled away, and I set off for my other life.

Chapter Eleven

I suppose it was inevitable that at some stage my two worlds would really collide. In a way, it was surprising it hadn't happened already. After all, I'd been seeing probably twenty men a week for over two years. Sooner or later I was bound to know one of them.

One night, Trish gave me details of a booking with a man called Jason. I was driving myself by now – I felt confident enough to do it, and it meant I took home an extra £100 or so that I had previously been giving Ant, which in turn offset the babysitting cost – and found the house easily enough.

I knocked on the door and waited.

After a moment, Jason opened it. He started, taking a half step backwards in shock, then just stared at me for a few seconds. I stared back, momentarily speechless. I was looking at a man I'd met three or four times socially, the last time just a couple of weeks ago at a Sunday lunch drinks party.

'Fuck me,' he said, shocked.

'Well, that's the general idea,' I said, lifting an eyebrow and giving him a smile.

I followed him into the sitting room and he poured me a drink.

'How long? Why? What the hell—' he began.

'Two years. I need the money. For the kids,' I replied simply. 'And you?' I asked, just a little archly. I clearly wasn't the only one operating a secret life. I knew he was married with children. I'd even met his wife. I wondered if she was one of those well-maintained expensive types who'd 'gone off sex'.

'Caroline's gone to stay with her mother. With the kids. We aren't terribly happy. It's not going very well at the moment.'

'You poor thing,' I said sympathetically. 'Shall we go upstairs?'

I knew I had to get him thinking beyond our social relationship if I wasn't about to lose the booking. And I didn't want to do that. In the end, it didn't matter that I knew Jason. It was still business as usual.

Jason led the way. Soon we stood in his bedroom, which was enormous.

'Shall we start with a massage?' I said.

From the way Jason looked at me, I knew he was getting over his shock and embarrassment and remembering why he'd booked me in the first place. Through his trousers I saw his cock rising.

'I've got some wonderful oil,' I added, swiftly unbuttoning my jacket to reveal my lacy black bra as I swung into my usual routine. Jason did as I suggested. I knew I was home and dry.

An hour later, we came downstairs again.

'That was fantastic,' Jason said.

'Wasn't it?' I murmured in agreement, as I always did. Half of what my clients needed was encouragement.

'Can we do it again?' he asked eagerly.

'Any time. Call the agency and ask for Elizabeth,' I told him, putting away the money he'd just given me. 'I look forward to it.'

I made to leave, then turned, with one final thought: 'Oh, one thing, Jason. This is our little secret, isn't it?'

'Oh God, yes,' said Jason, horrified at the very idea that his wife might find out what he was up to. He had at least as much to lose as I did. 'It's definitely our little secret.'

We smiled at each other, fellow conspirators, and I left.

I got into the car and turned on the engine. I had a feeling I had just acquired another regular.

With six children, it seemed that it was always someone's birthday. No sooner had I got one birthday behind me than I would have to start planning another. This time it was Alice's turn and as with all my kids' birthdays, I wanted to make a fuss of her. I knew what she wanted: a party at the local indoor play centre. So I duly booked the space and sent out the invitations. Of course I invited Paul; relations between us were amicable enough by now. He was, after all, the children's father.

That Saturday afternoon passed in a blur as forty children navigated their way around various bits of brightly coloured equipment, yelling at each other to 'come this way' or 'look at me'. The noise was so loud that it was almost impossible to hear, so the adults – a mix of parents, godparents and Paul and his family – stood miming at each other and smiling broadly, unable to communicate further. Meanwhile, the children, oblivious of the noise they were creating, were enjoying themselves hugely. Every now and then I caught a flash of my tomboy of a daughter dashing past to the next piece of climbing equipment, closely followed by several of her friends and siblings.

I glanced at Paul, standing next to me, nursing his cup of tea in silence. I was glad it was too noisy to talk. I didn't have anything I wanted to say. Paul and I had always communicated better without words.

I looked up and saw Alice climbing nimbly up the rope wall. She was nearly up at the top, with Alexander close behind. I felt a surge of pride as I watched. Whatever had happened between Paul and me, my children weren't doing so badly. They had a good, stable, fortunate life, they knew they were loved. My entire life was devoted to making sure they were all right, had what they needed, were hugged and kissed on a daily basis.

Uninvited, the memory of one of my own birthdays suddenly appeared in my mind. No party, and my father cornering me to give me my unwanted 'present'. I shook the thought from my mind. I had no time for the past now. I was too busy trying to stay afloat in the present, striving to be the best parent I knew how to be.

As I tucked Alice up that night and looked down at her lying snuggled under her duvet, I found it hard to believe that she was heading fast into her teens. I knew she wasn't going to be a little girl for much longer. Childhood was a precious and fleeting time; all the more reason, I felt convinced, to make it really special.

Later that evening the babysitter arrived, and I headed off to work, moving uneasily as usual from my home world to the world of work. I was tired from the busyness of the day. Alice, in her excitement, had got us all up at 6 a.m., and organising and running the party had taken it out of me. I just hoped the new client I was off to see would be straightforward. I didn't want to doze off on the job.

I knocked on the door and waited expectantly.

'Hello,' I said brightly when the door opened. The brightness tailed off slightly as I took in the vision in front of me. The punter was a very tall, well-built man with a beard, aged about fifty-five at a guess. His lips were painted a bright red, in a rather inexpert way, and he was wearing a dark, long-haired wig. I tried very hard not to look shocked as my eyes travelled the length of his body. He was wearing a little black satin baby-doll nightie, suspenders, stockings and high heels.

'Hello. Call me Gloria,' he smiled, red lips parting.

Upstairs, Gloria asked me to cuddle 'her'. 'She' wanted me to suckle her like a baby. So I found myself pretending to breastfeed this enormous middle-aged man for a while. After some time doing this, Gloria, clearly satisfied, stood up and undressed, revealing a powerful man's body with a huge erection.

'I'm Will,' he said, as if we had just met. More and more peculiar. 'Come and lie on the bed with me.'

So I did, wondering, Whatever next? This man clearly had a plot all of his own.

We lay side by side, and suddenly the bed started to vibrate.

'Isn't it marvellous?' Will chuckled, clearly delighted with his bed. 'It also heats itself up.'

Whatever next?

In a way, the most surprising element of the evening was that after such a bizarre beginning, we went on to have some shockingly straight sex. Gloria had become Will, and Will liked to do it in the missionary position.

Afterwards, I showered, said goodbye to Gloria/Will, and left. As I headed home to my reassuringly normal family set-up, I reflected that underneath the suspenders and lacy underwear, I was still the same person I'd always been. I was still capable of being shocked.

But if I thought that was shocking, I then encountered the worst moment of my escort life so far.

Rape had always been my worst nightmare. I knew how vulnerable I was when I was alone with a client inside their home, particularly now that I'd given up Ant and drove myself everywhere. Mostly, clients treated me well. But as in all walks of life, there were a few who didn't. I'd come across the odd client who was determined that I was a piece of dirt. 'You're just a fucking whore,' they'd say, 'a dirty piece of shit.' I'd bite my lip, and think, You're the tosser, because you're the one that's paying me.

When I met a client who treated me badly, I tried not to let it upset me. I knew why I was working as an escort, and I knew that it was for a good cause. I'd think of the old rhyme: sticks and stones may break my bones, but words will never hurt me. I'd take their money, the money that was saving my children's childhood, fuck them, and leave.

But this time, I met a client who thought that abusing me verbally wasn't enough.

It was a very hot Saturday in high summer. David had come over, and we'd just had a wonderful family day, splashing in the paddling pool and lazing about in the garden. I'd made ice lollies with the little ones, and we'd all eaten them after tea to cool down. Finally, I'd rather reluctantly got myself ready for work. The babysitter had arrived, I'd kissed the kids goodnight, and set off.

My night was already mapped out for me. My first job was in Brighton, not too far away, an easy drive. Then I was to go on to a regular, also in Brighton, for the rest of the evening. It was a regular I liked, who treated me well and always gave me a tip, who usually gave me a glass of ice-cold champagne and a delicious supper before we adjourned upstairs. As I sped along singing along to Abba, I felt that at least I had a relatively easy night ahead of me.

So my spirits were quite good as I drove in the direction of my first booking. Now that I didn't have Ant, I'd bought maps to all the nearby towns and rarely got lost. In fact I knew Southern England about as well as the lines on my face by now. I quickly found the house and parked. I took out my bag, and walked up to the door.

I looked at my watch. Eight o'clock. I had just an hour's booking here, and then I was off to my regular. I rang the bell.

A well-built fair-haired man opened the door.

'Come in,' he said, unsmiling. I stepped over the threshold not knowing, not even suspecting, that I was walking into every call girl's nightmare.

He slammed the door behind me and leant against it.

My stomach flipped over.

'Can we get the money side of things out of the way first?' I asked pleasantly, hoping there was no revealing tremble in my voice.

'Later,' he growled. 'Upstairs.' He pushed me in the direction of the stairs. I felt scared, but what choice did I have? I moved in the direction he indicated. At the top of the stairs, he pushed me towards an open door.

'In there.'

The room held a double bed and not much else. I turned to look at the client. He was right behind me. With a shove, I was on the bed on my back.

'You whore,' he snarled. 'You deserve this.' And with that he punched me in the face. I struggled, my head reeling, and he hit me again. He trapped me with his body, lying on top of me, hauling at my clothing, fumbling with his fly. He was so much bigger than me that I couldn't escape. I knew he was going to rape me and I just prayed for it to be over. I prayed that I would survive.

I lay with my eyes closed, trying to shut out what was happening to me. Insults washed over me in an endless torrent of abuse: 'You filthy little tart – you're scum, you are, you're filth.'

I felt my knickers rip. He pushed my legs apart, and then, after more fumbling, I felt him force himself into me. At the same time he was still insulting me wildly: 'You filthy bitch, you're such a dirty little tart.'

Finally it was over. He rolled off me and sat up. He was pulling at the condom on his penis. Thank God, I thought. He used a condom.

'Right. That's it. Get dressed, you tart.'

I'd never had the chance to get undressed, but I scuttled off the bed like a wounded beetle heading for cover, and rearranged my torn clothing. The man was counting out some notes. He threw them towards me. 'Now fuck off,' he said. 'Just fuck off.'

I picked up the money and ran down the stairs, terrified as I pounded down every step that it was a joke, that he would change his mind, that he was toying with me. Would I feel him grab me from behind any second? I reached the bottom and snatched up my bag, which was still sitting by the front door where I had left it. I turned the latch and pulled frantically. Please, please don't let it be locked. I didn't want it to be locked. I didn't want to struggle with the door, I didn't want to look up and see the man at the top of the stairs, belt or hammer in hand, a sick, powerful smile spreading slowly across his face. I didn't want to be trapped and crushed like a butterfly. I wanted only to get home to my children, to safety.

All these panicky thoughts flashed through my mind in a splinter of a second. Then the door opened easily, there was no man at the top of the stairs, and I was outside again, running for my car.

I got in shakily and locked the doors from the inside, fumbled for the keys, started the engine, and drove off erratically down the street. I was headed anywhere – I just had to get away. I was trembling, gripping the steering wheel tightly to stop my hands shaking. Then the shock of what had happened to me began to sink in. I caught sight of my face in the rear-view mirror. My right cheek was reddening with a fast-coming bruise. My wrists bore the purple imprints of the man's hands where he had held me down. My body ached all over.

After ten minutes of wild, directionless driving, I pulled over on to the side of a residential street. I forced myself to take some deep breaths. I had to calm down.

I got some tissues out of my handbag and dampened one with some bottled water. I dabbed at my injuries as best I could. Then I took out my phone and rang the agency.

'Trish,' I said, holding back the tears that threatened to overwhelm me. I felt ten years old. 'Trish, I've just been raped.'

'Oh God. Oh no,' Trish said. The horror she felt rang through her voice.

We were both silent for a moment. Then she took charge. Sympathetic and calming, she cancelled my regular and told me to go home. 'You poor darling,' she said, turning her horror into fury with the client who had done this to me. 'The bastard.'

I knew that Trish would never take a booking from him again. We also both knew there was no point even mentioning the police.

'Thanks, Trish,' I sniffed, after a few more comforting words.

I started the engine again, and set off slowly in the direction of home.

I drove along, my skin crawling. I felt really dirty. I wanted to stop and have a wash before I got home. I didn't want the children, the older ones who might still be up, to see me like this, so I pulled in at the next service station and tried to tidy myself up in the cloakroom. I combed my wild and rumpled hair into a semblance of order. My scalp hurt so much where he had pulled hard on my hair that I wondered if clumps were missing. I took out my foundation compact and tried to cover up the bruise on my cheek. Even with the help of make-up it stood out on my cheek for what it was – a bruise. My attempts to disguise it were further hindered by the tears I was fighting to stop streaking down my face. I blew my nose for the thousandth time. 'Get a grip,' I told myself. 'Get a grip.'

I looked again at the badly covered-up bruise. I'd have to think of something to explain it. But what? I fell against the photocopier? I walked into a bookshelf?

I jumped as someone pushed open the door and came into the washroom. Did she give me a funny look, or was I just being paranoid? I couldn't decide. My heart was thundering in my ears again, thump, thump, thump, as if to warn me against approaching danger. I was in a state. I took a couple of deep breaths. I had to get home.

I bought a strong takeaway coffee and went back to the car. Within half an hour I was pulling up outside my house. I felt too battered by events to take my suitcase home to Sarah tonight; it would have to stay in the boot of the car. It would be safe for just one night. Nobody would find it.

I looked at my watch. Nearly ten p.m. The summer sky was only just now darkening to deep blue. Was it really less than three hours ago that I'd been setting off for work with a light heart? Four hours ago that I was licking home-made ice lollies in the garden, a wet, swimming-costume-clad Victoria on my knee? Five hours ago that I was kissing David, soaking wet, after he'd pushed me in the paddling pool? How could such a perfect day end with an event of such horror? But wasn't that the awful unpredictability of life?

Trying to rein in the threads of my increasingly rambling thoughts, I let myself into the house. Hattie was babysitting tonight, and she came out into the hall to see who it was.

'Hello,' I said, hardly able to manage a smile.

'What's happened to you?' she asked, horrified, taking in my face with a swift glance.

'I took a bit of a fall at work,' I lied. 'On to the photocopier. Tripped on an edge of carpet just by it. Health and Safety has been meaning to fix it for weeks. They've sent me home. I'm just going to go and have a bath and lie down. Feeling a bit groggy,' I explained, fleeing upstairs.

I needed peace. Solitude. Not to have to explain anything to anyone.

And I needed to get clean.

He had been really rough, I reflected, as I sat in the steaming bath counting my bruises. Sinking back under the comforting cloak of warm water, I thanked my lucky stars that he hadn't been a complete maniac. I was lucky to be alive.

Going back to work after that was very, very hard. How I longed then for a man to take care of me, to put his arms round me and say, 'It's all right, darling, I'll look after you. Just leave the bills to me.'

But after a few days my bruises had faded, and only the memory of the rape remained. There was no longer a reason not to return to work. I had to face it.

As I bathed and dressed in preparation for my first night back, my thoughts swirled about, leaving streaks of colour across my bleak, black mind. How inconsequential I was, just one of an endless tide of women down the ages who had, like me, been forced to take up prostitution to make ends meet. In that way, the twenty-first century was surprisingly unadvanced. Whatever promises men made, whatever safety net the state supposedly offered, too often women ended up fending for themselves and their children on their own.

I knew I wasn't the first mother to leave her kids each night to go and make money to pay for their existence. Prostitution was one of the oldest trades there was; for thousands of years, women like me had left their children to go out and sell themselves to make a living; to put food on the table, clothes on their children's backs. Nineteenth-century Paris was just one good example of this, better known than many other periods because of the painters who immortalised the prostitutes of the time on their canvases. Degas dressed them up as ballet dancers, Toulouse

Lautrec painted one as a cabaret dancer, and even personalised her by giving her the name of 'Jane Avril'. But the veneer was transparent: everyone knew the artists had been painting street girls. Who, I wondered wearily, as I did up my lacy black bra, had they left their children with as they went out night after night to do what they simply had to do to survive? Perhaps they grouped together, drew up a rota, having a night off in turn and minding each other's children?

Silently I finished dressing and prepared to leave. I kissed my children goodbye and went outside to my other life once again, shutting the door more reluctantly than ever before. As I climbed into the car, I dared to ask myself the question – to face and perhaps even answer the question – that I had been dodging for some time now.

How much longer could I do this job?

As long as we need the money, my head replied sharply, driving me on to ever greater efforts. Work harder, sleep with more men, earn more, save more.

Not much longer. Not that much longer, whispered my heart, my spirit, my soul.

Now I was more careful than ever before. I followed Simon's advice to the letter. I left my car unlocked, with a set of spare keys in the driver's side in case the client took my handbag. I only wore shoes with ankle straps, and I kept my jewellery to a minimum.

I preferred it when Trish was working the phones. I knew she checked the clients really thoroughly, calling them back to make sure they were who they said they were, and letting me know if they were new to the agency. I knew from experience that Holly, who owned the business and was determined to accept every booking, sometimes told me a client had used the agency before when they hadn't.

The rape had made me aware of all the risks, and I don't mean just the risks that threatened me. It had also rather belatedly dawned on me what ludicrous risks many of my clients took. Some of my clients, men at the top of their professional ladders, paid me with credit cards or cheques. If I'd been the type to sell my story to a tabloid, I doubt it would have taken me long to ignite an editor's interest with the proof I had to back up my claims. I could even see the headlines: JUDGE IN SEX SCANDAL WITH PVC-CLAD ESCORT GIRL.

It was a fact of my working life that some of the people who booked me were drawn from the great and the good of the day: the top barristers, solicitors, accountants, the judges, the city bankers, the chief executives of the multinationals. In short, some of the so-called pillars of our society. Men who were perceived as an example to us all, who were regularly considered newsworthy for the purported value of the various contributions they made to the world, were amongst those who rang the agency and booked to see me. They weren't famous exactly, but they were very high-profile.

High-profile men don't want to be caught having sex with a hooker. It's not exactly a good career move. So why did they take such ludicrous risks? And since they did, why did they enhance the risk by paying with cheques or credit cards, giving me hard evidence to support my story if I wanted to spill the beans? I would never even have considered this – I'd taken a decision to sell myself, not other people – but I don't think all prostitutes are always quite so clear on this point.

It is something that remains a mystery to me to this day. Was the sex really worth it? Were they *so* lonely that they just didn't care what they potentially stood to lose? The answer probably varied from case to case; and in truth it doesn't matter that, hard as I tried, I couldn't fathom it out. These men were just lucky they were having paid sex with me rather than someone who might have been interested in sharing their experiences with a reader-ship of two million. I couldn't have cared less how important they were. My interest was the money. They were willing to pay and treated me well. No questions asked, discretion guaranteed.

Sam, however, was an exception – the only high-flying client I came anywhere near to understanding.

A barrister at the top of his profession, Sam wasn't famous exactly, but he was nevertheless very well known within his field. He'd been a key player in a number of high-profile cases, and even I, who don't follow the law pages of the broadsheets, had heard of him.

I always visited Sam in his apartment. He opened the door that first Saturday night in a crisp white shirt and a tight pair of worn-looking jeans, a tall, good-looking man fast approaching fifty who obviously took good care of himself. I knew who he was from the moment he introduced himself, which he did as if we

244

were meeting at a party, smiling into my eyes, shaking my hand.

A few moments later, I lay on his bed in my scanty underwear, holding in my stomach as Sam stripped off, revealing his well-kept body. Why, I wondered – as I occasionally had before when I had come across the kind of man most women would kill to go out with – would a man with a body, a brain, and a salary like Sam's pay for sex? Why did he need to, and why would he, with such a high-flying career at stake, take such a massive risk?

Sam felt my eyes on him, and turned towards me, naked.

'Come here,' I invited, and he did, crawling across the bed towards me.

First I massaged his back, and then I turned him over, straddling him at waist height, and began to massage his front. I could feel his well-worked muscles between my fingers, and his cock was ramrod hard beneath me. His eyes were shut, his mouth curved upwards in a very slight smile. I could tell that despite the pleasure he was in complete control. I imagined him in a courtroom in his wig and gown – something Sam and I had in common: we both dressed up for a living – exercising that same control in different circumstances; charming the jury, making his point in a way that was eloquent but deadly. It was clear he was a very powerful man.

I started to kiss his chest, working my way down his body. As I got nearer and nearer to his cock, he murmured, 'God, you're gorgeous.'

It was rather sweet. I was hardly a woman who needed to be persuaded with compliments. Having been booked, I was a sure thing.

After that first encounter, he booked me every Saturday night. He paid me by cheque, but was so regular a client it might as well have been by standing order. I'd turn up about eleven o'clock every Saturday, and would generally stay a couple of hours. Most of the time was spent in bed. After sex, we'd chat, about his work, about world events, and often about books. We had discovered that we were both avid readers. Sam was keen on dark, tightly plotted thrillers, while I was willing to read anything and everything,

He was so normal, so bright, so interesting, so successful, that eventually I just had to ask him why on earth he wanted to keep booking me.

'Why don't you get yourself a wife?' I asked incredulously, wrinkling my brow. 'I can't believe you're short of offers.'

His face split into a wonderful smile, as if I had cracked a hilarious joke.

'You're a great deal cheaper than a wife, Elizabeth,' he replied.

He may have been smiling, but I knew immediately that he was completely serious. £500 a week spent on me was nothing compared with the cost of a house, a second car, a wife's maintenance bills, not to mention the cost of any kids that came along. But Sam wasn't talking only about the financial cost of a relationship. There was something else besides.

'I don't want to get married. I don't want kids. I'm a doting uncle to my nephews and nieces, but I don't want my own. So why risk getting entangled?' he explained.

It was the risk of the messy personal life that made Sam turn to someone like me. Even the thought of being outed as some-one who had sex with a prostitute – a risk he must have considered, he who looked at every angle of a situation for a living – was obviously preferable to him than the daily demands of a relationship and the risk that it might all go wrong. I won-dered what it was that had scarred Sam, left him too scared to get properly involved. Had his parents divorced? Had he been mar-ried before? I couldn't ask, and Sam didn't see the need to tell me.

So I accepted his explanation, and the weekly booking con-tinued. I was Sam's company, on tap, once a week. I was his Saturday-night date. He worked hard the rest of the time, and as a result was a highly successful lawyer, something which obviously gave him immense satisfaction. For Sam, at least, it was a good enough life balance.

The weeks were rolling by fast now. Suddenly the endless summer holiday was practically over, and the autumn term loomed yet again. It was time to start looking out the uniforms, the hockey sticks, the football boots, and to assemble it all into some sort of order.

One morning, a few days before term was due to begin, I looked round the breakfast table at my children and realised how brown and healthy they were looking. Several weeks of unstructured life, time spent mucking about in the garden, in the woods, walking Scooby, seeing friends, had given them all a relaxed, easy glow. But it was time to lick them into shape for school again. They all needed a haircut – Alexander could barely see out from under his fringe – and of course, as part of that back-to-school ritual, I needed to get their teeth checked. I picked up the phone to make the appointments, to the accompaniment of loud groans and cries of 'Oh, Mum!' Much as I, too, wanted to carry on living those long, enjoyable summer days, I knew we had to face reality.

I'd discovered early on in motherhood that taking children to the hairdresser was about as appealing a proposition as having your fingernails extracted without anaesthetic. So I'd found a gem of a woman called Jo, a hairdresser who came to the house. I'd used her for years now, and when I rang to book her, she always blocked out an afternoon. After all, there were seven haircuts to do.

The dentist was probably one of the only remaining links to my childhood. Mr Brown had looked after my teeth all my life, and now I took my children to him. He had an easy manner with them, giving them rides up and down in his chair, and the combination of his care and my insistence on regular brushing meant that not one of the children yet had a filling.

One afternoon a few days later, we all filed into Mr Brown's waiting room. He looked over the children one by one, in a visit as uneventful as usual. Afterwards, as was our family custom, we went to the baker's next door to buy doughnuts. Not ideal snacks following a visit to the dentist, but something of a ritual for us. With no fillings, I felt I could afford to be lenient a couple of times a year.

Soon the autumn term was in full swing. The weeks were full of school and play dates and clubs, and the weekends always busy fitting in the children's various hobbies. Ice skating or roller skating was a hit with all the children, as was a trip to the cinema, where, between us, we'd take up almost a whole row. Scooby always needed a walk, and cheering Alexander on at rugby on Sunday mornings had practically become a family institution.

September was also the month of Victoria's birthday, and I found myself organising a trampoline party for all her class. My youngest daughter, following in Alice's footsteps, was now turning into quite a little tomboy herself. A heart murmur and 40 per cent hearing didn't seem to stop her from living life to the full; she was passionate about everything outdoors: skateboarding, doing wheelies on her BMX bike, climbing trees, swimming in the sea. I'd given up trying to coax her into a dress, and generally bought her clothes from the boys' section at Gap. I admired her courage at getting on with life.

Everything was going well. I was tired – I'd never meant to work so long or so hard – but on the domestic front the children were happy, and my babysitting routine was still working smoothly. David was loving and attentive, and often chose to join in our family activities. When he brought his children too, I really would have a gang on my hands with eight kids in the house. I didn't mind. I enjoyed the happiness, the noise, the laughter. It was everything I'd always wanted.

Just one thing niggled at me. Maybe the rape had left me

paranoid, but I kept having the strangest sensation that I was being followed. It was a feeling that sneaked up on me when I was least expecting it. But now the thought had taken root in my mind, it was one that I found hard to dismiss.

I kept seeing the same car, again and again. A pale green Peugeot saloon. I'd noticed it several times on the way over to Sarah's to collect my case each evening; I'd spotted it seemingly following me as I went into town one afternoon to do some errands; I'd seen it drive past me the other day as I was collecting the children from school.

One evening, I was out with David when I noticed that the Peugeot had mysteriously appeared behind us.

'David,' I said, 'I've got a really weird feeling I'm being followed.'

I didn't want to say too much – how could I tell David that I was scared it might be a mad client who'd raped me, when he thought I worked in a document word-processing centre? – but I had to tell him something. He was such a part of my life now, and I was starting to rely on him. I had to tell him my fears.

He threw me a strange look. 'Followed? Why? Who by? Could it be Paul?'

That was a thought that hadn't occurred to me. But why? Paul knew about David and me. He didn't like it, but he knew. What could he be hoping to find out about me that he didn't already know?

David didn't wait long for an answer I couldn't give. 'Don't worry, I'll lose him,' he said, and put his foot down.

For the next ten minutes, David whizzed and turned down a

series of back routes, while I kept my eye on the Peugeot. Within minutes it had gone.

'We've lost him,' I said, pleased.

As I settled back in my seat, David put his hand on my knee. 'There,' he said. 'Nothing to worry about.'

I glanced at him suspiciously. He was humouring me, I could tell.

'You think I'm making it up, don't you?' I said. 'Well, you're wrong. I've seen that car all round town the last couple of weeks.'

'Whatever you say, darling,' David grinned, parking outside the restaurant where we were headed. He leaned over and kissed me. I couldn't be cross with him for long.

'I'm telling you, it was following me,' I grumbled, as he helped me out of the car. But maybe David was right. Maybe I was imagining things. Hand in hand, we went inside to dinner.

Over the next few days, I found I was looking out for the green car wherever I went. I realised I was looking for it on the school run, in the supermarket car park, in town when I went to get my nails done. But it was nowhere to be seen. Then, just as I was starting to relax, to think that David was right, something strange happened that made me wonder whether it might not be my imagination after all.

I got back from the school run to find the post on the mat. I picked it up and took it into the kitchen, where the usual debris of breakfast awaited me. I put the kettle on to make a cup of tea, and tidied up while I waited for it to boil. Then I skimmed through the letters. A couple of junk items went straight in the bin, and there was a postcard to the kids from Terry and Jan, who were on holiday. There was a bill, which, under the new regime, I opened and dealt with immediately. And there was an official-looking letter. I opened it and began to read. It was from the National Insurance people.

'Following your enquiry regarding your lost National Insurance number . . .' it began.

I paused. What enquiry? I knew I hadn't made any such enquiry. Surely it must be a mistake.

Unless . . . What if someone else had?

Suddenly, I knew with a flash of instinct that I was right. Someone was following me, or having me followed. And that was only part of it – they were also probing into the details of my life.

But who? And why?

Baffled, I rang the number on the top of the letter in a bid to find out more. I explained the curious situation I found myself in to the girl who answered. After finding my file on the computer, she was adamant that the letter was a response to a request for my National Insurance number, a request that had been made by someone claiming to be me, over the phone.

'It couldn't be a mistake?' I asked.

'No. Absolutely not,' she said. 'If it had been a computer-generated letter sent out to everyone, possibly. But this isn't a computer-generated letter – it's a direct response to an individual situation. You – or someone pretending to be you – rang and asked for your National Insurance number. The letter you are holding is the written confirmation of that request.'

My brain whirred. It definitely hadn't been me, which meant that someone else had rung up. What that person hadn't realised was that their enquiry had led to this letter, alerting me to the fact that something strange was going on.

'Why would anyone want to have my National Insurance number?' I asked her, mystified. 'What can you do with it?'

'Oh, lots of things,' she told me eagerly, as if she was glad to be able to be of some help to me on this, at least. 'It can get you access to a person's tax records, for a start. And of course on the tax records there would be several personal details: a person's full name and address, their occupation, how much they'd earned that year, that kind of thing.'

It didn't take long for the implications of this to sink in. It was likely that whoever was following me was very probably the same person who had tried to get my National Insurance number. That meant they had my full address, and an idea of how much I earned. Obviously I didn't put 'call girl' as my occupation on my tax records, but I did declare every penny I earned. Whoever was interested in the details of my life would see instantly that a night job at a word-processing centre wouldn't pay anything like the sums I'd earned in the last two years. Their next question would be, 'So what is she really doing for a living?'

But who would go to such lengths to find out what I was really up to? I didn't think it could be Paul – I was as sure as I could be that he had absolutely no idea that I didn't do the job I claimed to do. And the way he was at the moment, he wouldn't smell a rat unless I swung it under his nose. The mothers at school were

253

more likely to get suspicious of my lifestyle than Paul. Now I thought about it, one or two of them had commented a couple of times on how well I was managing since Paul and I had split up. I'd shrugged it off at the time, hinting that I'd divorced well, hoping that that would satisfy their curiosity. But perhaps it hadn't? Perhaps a mother at school was trying to find out more about me? I shook my head in disbelief. No, that didn't make any sense at all.

No. It had to be the client who had raped me. I simply couldn't think of anyone else who'd go to such lengths.

This thought horrified me. Had I, by my decision to become an escort, now put my life in danger? And what about my children? How mad was this client turned stalker? Would he want to hurt them, too? And what could I do? I could hardly call the police. I certainly couldn't tell David. I was on my own with this. I had to think of some way to sort it out before something dreadful happened.

Then one more thought struck me. In a way, it was even more dreadful than the thought that I might have a dangerous rapist on my tail. What if . . . I could hardly entertain the thought. What if the person snooping into my life wasn't the rapist after all? What if it was someone much closer to home? Like – my heart turned to stone – David?

I didn't want to face it, but I had to. After all, it wasn't so far-fetched an idea. My brain was whizzing like a fruit machine, and it kept coming up with three cherries. There was his continual interest in my work. There were his remarks about how much I earned. He had noticed that I was extremely highly paid for a secretary, even one who worked such antisocial shifts. Now he was so involved in our lives that he had had every opportunity to notice the more luxurious things we had: the DVD player, the trampoline out the back, the extra music lessons for the children. With our backlog of debts now paid off, our consumption had become a little more conspicuous. We had more cash to spend.

Oh no, please don't let it be David. Of course I didn't want it to be the rapist; I certainly didn't want me or the children to be at risk. But I couldn't bear it to be David either.

There had to be another explanation. After all, I reminded myself, why would he have tried so hard to lose the car I thought had been following me the other night? No, I told myself, quite adamant now; it couldn't be him. I just had to keep racking my brains, and I'd come up with the right answer in the end.

All the same, I felt a chill tiptoe its way icily down my spine.

Chapter Twelve

*I*t felt like fear was all around me, marching towards me like a thousand-strong army, crowding round me, closer and closer, squeezing me into a corner. I could see only one way to puncture the unspoken, formless threat that I could sense but not see. It centred on a decision that I longed to take, that had been growing ever more prominent in my thoughts since I had been raped.

I wanted to give up work.

The idea of not getting dressed night after night to head off into the unknown to have sex with nameless, faceless individuals was increasingly tantalising. I imagined long evenings at home: no more rushing to finish homework; I could have supper with the children every night. David and I might occasionally go out to the cinema or for supper. Other nights we could cosy up together on the sofa.

I tortured myself with these fantasies until, finally, I sat down one afternoon and drew up a list of reasons to stop working set against reasons why I should continue. The column in favour of giving up filled incredibly quickly: I'd paid off our backlog of debts and was up to date with our outgoings; the credit cards were cleared, the mortgage was back on a regular footing and my current account was in credit – I had even started to build up some savings; I was exhausted and had worked much longer than I had ever intended; I was definitely being followed, meaning it was surely a matter of time before someone else discovered what I was up to, and I'd like to get out before that happened if I possibly could; I could spend more time with David and the kids; finally – I underlined this three times – as a human being, as a person in my own right, rather than as a mother, a carer and sole provider, I just longed to stop with every fibre of my being.

My pen moved on to the second column, hovering there while I thought for a moment. It took me just seconds to realise that however I approached it, there was and only ever had been just one reason to continue. There were no career prospects in this job. I was not going to get a promotion, an offer of a partnership or a pay rise; it was the same work, night after night. I wasn't in it for job satisfaction. The reason was money. As I wrote the word down, I could feel that it didn't carry anything like the weight it had three years ago when I had made that first tentative call to Jimmy.

Because I had worked so hard for so long, our circumstances had completely recovered. I knew that if I dared, I could stop – and soon. I desperately wanted to. I simply had to think of some other way to support all of us, to prevent us sliding back into terrible debt. I had worked so hard to scramble back up out of the landslide of debt that had nearly swept away my family's whole life that I was terrified of ever going back there. The big question was, if I stopped, would the bills quickly mount up again? I knew the answer was a resounding yes, unless I could find another way to earn enough money to pay them.

Clearly I couldn't work like this for ever. In fact, I didn't think I had it in me to carry on for very much longer at all. I looked at the statement detailing the amount I had saved, and got out the calculator. I worked out that with our current outgoings, my savings would last three months. It wasn't long enough. Three months could easily fly by without my coming up with an alternative income stream.

But if I worked for just one more month, I could earn enough to give us a buffer of six months. And surely in six months I could find a different way to support us all?

I shut my notebook and put it back in the kitchen drawer where I kept all my financial notes and correspondence. I had decided. One more month, working as hard as I could to give us all some security once I'd stopped, and that would be it. That decision seemed a good marriage of the financial and the emotional – what we needed, and what I could give. I felt both liberated and motivated at the same time. The idea of having a date to stop made my heart lift. Just one more month, I told myself. Hang on for just one more month. One little month, after nearly two and a half years of working: what difference could that make?

As it turned out, a great deal. If my life was a row of dominoes, well, somebody had just flicked over the first domino in the line. And that little flick was enough: a chain reaction had begun. I didn't know it yet, but the fiction that was my working life was about to come crashing down, piece by piece. Working that last month changed everything.

The knowledge that I wouldn't be doing this job in a month's time spurred me on to a final burst. I was on the brink of retirement, I told myself: why not, in these last few weeks, take absolutely every client who came my way? Yes, it was grim, yes, it was exhausting, awful, degrading. But if it meant a little longer at the other end without worrying about how I was going to keep us all, wasn't it worth it?

Yes. So I worked harder than ever.

A few days later, at two in the morning, I drew up outside a rather prestigious car dealership. I was meeting a new client, Gavin. I parked my car close to the front door of the vast showroom, and got out. The street lamps were broken and it was very dark. I pulled my coat closer around me against a chill wind and reflected how much, at times like this, I really missed Ant – not only the security he'd offered, but also the company. It was very lonely, driving from place to place, turning up on a stranger's doorstep with a painted-on smile and my bag of tricks.

Buck up, I told myself. Look on the bright side: I could find my way round the M25 and the surrounding area with a blindfold on.

I was trying to make myself laugh; I couldn't afford to lose heart quite yet. I took my bag out of the boot, slammed it shut and walked towards what looked like the front door. I was only halfway there when it swung open.

A short, cheery-looking man with receding, sandy-coloured hair stood in the doorway, illuminated by the light coming from inside.

'Hello,' he said, 'I'm Gavin.'

'Call me Elizabeth,' I replied, thinking to myself: But not for much longer.

Gavin ushered me inside. We were in a showroom full of extremely expensive-looking 4×4s.

'Nice cars,' I said, looking around me. 'Very nice.'

Gavin started to tell me about them, outlining all their special features. He was clearly very enthusiastic about his job. Words like 'in-car entertainment' and 'air bag' drifted over me as I focused on a car just two away from me. It was the perfect family car, one I had recently been coveting. An automatic 4×4 with seven seats, in dark green, safe as a house on wheels. It simply couldn't be improved on.

I shut my mind and went about my work. Soon I was reclining, semi-naked, on the bonnet of a 4×4, as if I was a model in one of the less tasteful car advertisements, while Gavin stared as if he'd won the lottery. From the growing bulge in his trousers, acting out his fantasy was proving to be successful. I could see he was getting quite worked up. I slid down the bonnet a bit, terrified of scratching the paintwork with the clips on my suspender belt.

'Why don't you come a little closer,' I suggested. I could see he was just longing to fuck me up against the car.

Gavin didn't require a second invitation. As he moved up against me, I undid his fly. 'Let's see what we can do for you, shall we?' I said, releasing his cock from the prison of his underpants through his open trouser fly with one expert hand. I'd done this movement so often by now I was surprised I hadn't got RSI. Lots of men loved to fuck semi-clothed, as if they were in a hurry, doing something illicit, as if there was a risk they might get caught.

Later we adjourned to the sofa in the sales room, more often used for clients to sit on while waiting for service.

'Fantastic,' Gavin breathed, flat on his back on the sofa, naked, having just come for the second time. 'That was fantastic.'

Smiling, satisfied, he settled up with me, and, dressed again, started to walk me back towards the door.

'I could do with a new car,' I joked, as I turned to say goodbye, 'mine's absolutely falling to bits.'

Instantly Gavin was back in salesman mode. 'Really?' he said. 'Which one would you like?'

In a flash, I was pointing to the seven-seater four-wheel drive I'd been admiring earlier. 'My dream car,' I said. 'Ever since I saw it on *Top Gear*.'

'Instalments?' Gavin suggested. 'I could give you a good discount and very soft repayment terms, since we're . . . friends.'

Four days later, my new 4×4 stood in the drive.

Saturday got off to a slow start. The children were pottering around the house, doing their homework, playing in the garden, while I was clearing up the scattered debris of our leisurely breakfast. Scooby lay in his basket beside me, chewing idly on an Action Man; Victoria was kneeling up at the table making a 'potion' out of half the contents of the grocery cupboard. I had just made a cup of coffee, and was reflecting on how nice it was not to have to rush for a change, when the doorbell rang.

I wasn't expecting anyone, apart from David, who had said he'd come with his children in time for lunch. I glanced at the kitchen clock – it was only twenty to ten. I pulled my dressing gown cord tighter – I had yet to get dressed – and went to answer it.

'Nigel,' I said. 'Hello.' Nigel was the husband of Jane, a woman I'd met years ago with whom I'd stayed in touch. I didn't know Nigel well. Now I felt slightly nonplussed. I wondered what he wanted.

'I'd just like a word, if I may,' he said pleasantly.

'Of course. Come in,' I said.

As we walked through to the sitting room, he said hello to Jack and Charlotte, who were heading back to the playroom with a packet of biscuits they'd obviously filched from the kitchen while I wasn't looking. When they saw me, their faces fell, dismayed at being caught red-handed. But there were worse crimes small children could be committing on an autumn Saturday morning, in my opinion, so I just laughed at them, wagging my finger teasingly.

'Don't eat them all at once, kids,' I pretended to scold, and they ran off clutching the pack and giggling triumphantly before I could change my mind.

'Have a seat. What can I do for you?' I asked as I closed the sitting-room door.

Nigel smiled at me then. A slightly unpleasant smile.

'I know what you're up to,' he said.

I frowned at him, puzzled. 'What are you talking about?' I asked. I really had no idea.

'I know you're a hooker, and I want some,' Nigel said.

I had bare seconds to wonder if Nigel was my stalker before he was upon me. 'Just this once and I won't tell a soul,' he said. He was pushing me against the wall by the fireplace and reaching under my dressing gown.

'Don't scream, your kids are next door,' he muttered, shoving into me.

And so I was helpless. Soundlessly, Nigel took what he wanted, and left.

Stunned, I crumpled on to the sofa, curling my feet underneath me. My head felt as if there was a terrible pressure building up inside it. I wanted to cry. I thought that might relieve it, but my eyes were as dry as dust. I could hardly take it in: I had been raped again. This time by someone I knew. And there was nothing I could do about it. Jane was a great friend of mine. How could I tell her that her husband had just raped me? And as before, the police weren't an option. I knew that the minute Nigel told them I was a working girl, they'd laugh in my face. That would just result in more humiliation. No, there was no one to tell. No one who could help me. It was a horribly familiar feeling, one that cast me back years. As I dragged myself upstairs to run a scalding hot bath in a bid to eliminate the memory of Nigel's touch, I felt as I had all those years ago, living with my father. Afraid, alone, and trying very hard to pretend it was happening to someone else.

I locked the bathroom door behind me and turned on the taps, squirting in some rose essence. I looked in the mirror at my face. How could it look as it always did after what had just happened? It revealed nothing of what I was feeling. There was nothing to indicate the pain running through my body. Once again I wished I could cry; I just felt it might help. But my eyes stared back at me, tired and dry. It was years too late for tears. The crying should have started when I was a young girl, the first time I had been forced to have sex against my will. But I hadn't cried then, and it didn't look like I was going to start now all these years later.

I climbed into the rose-fragranced bath, dry-eyed, aching, wondering what it was about me that invited men to take what they wanted as if I was a rag doll with no feelings or preferences of my own. Would this go on happening to me for the rest of my life? Would I ever feel safe again?

The warmth of the water stole its way around me. I inhaled the smell of roses and felt a little calmer. Rose, I recalled from somewhere, was traditionally used for healing purposes.

I lay in silence for a moment. Then there was a knock at the door.

'Mummy?' a little voice demanded. 'Are you in there?'

It was Jack.

'I'm having a bath, darling.'

'Can I come in?'

I sighed, then got out and unlocked the door.

Jack looked at me. I was covered in bubbles. I climbed back in the bath.

'Mummy,' he said, his little face shining with hope and excitement, 'can we go and see the new Harry Potter film this afternoon?'

An image flashed into my mind. I saw myself in the middle of a cinema row, surrounded by my six kids, all of us munching from our pots of popcorn. As I pictured us on our outing, a calmness crept over me. Despite it all, I was lucky. I still had my family. I felt a surge of gratitude to my kids then as I realised that in spite of all the horribleness life had to offer, they somehow made me feel safe. My six wonderful children, with their needs, their fears, their hopes, their dreams, gave me my place in the world, my sense of purpose, my whole reason to exist, to go on battling against whatever life threw at me. With them to think of, I would always manage to pick myself up and fight another round in the ring of life. I might be bruised, tired, unable to cry, but suddenly I was no longer afraid.

'Come here and have a wet hug, sweetie,' I said, stretching out wet, soapy arms to my little boy. He pottered across the room and I held him close. I flicked some bubbles at him, making him laugh, and added, 'And of course we can go to Harry Potter, darling. It's a brilliant idea.'

I drove myself even harder as the day when I would stop work for ever drew nearer. Suddenly I was halfway through – I was seeing all my regulars each week, allowing myself to mentally count down our last visits. I had decided I would only tell them I was giving up at the last visit. I was also seeing any new clients who came my way. Every night I had found myself still out at work as the sun came up, squeezing in one final client.

That Sunday morning, at about 4 a.m., I went to my last booking of the night at an apartment in the Docklands area in London. The door swung open to reveal a solid man in his mid-twenties who looked like a prop forward. He was wearing a shirt with an obvious wine stain down the front, and a pair of jeans.

'Hi, I'm Richard,' he said. 'Welcome. Come in.' And he flung an arm wide in the direction of the interior of the apartment as if he was a traffic cop. He was clearly drunk, and taking a closer look at his eyes, very possibly charlied up. Pupils the size of Jaffa cakes, I observed. That certainly indicated drug consumption of some kind or other.

Oh God, I thought, tired to my bones. I'd already seen Sam and two other clients tonight. Just what I needed – a client who'd take ages to come. Never mind, I was here now. Think of the money.

The apartment was one vast sitting-room-cum-kitchen, with old oak floors, exposed brick walls and little furniture. It looked as if he'd just moved in, but he told me that actually he was a fan of the minimalist look and he'd been living there for over four years. He was about to get married, he said, in a week's time, and I was his final bachelor boy fling.

We went through to the bedroom, and I quickly undressed down to my underwear.

'Why don't you undress and we'll start with a massage?' I suggested, as was my habit.

Richard pulled his rugby shirt off with one swift movement. I had expected a rugby player's body, perhaps a hairy chest – he certainly had a lot of dark stubble on his face. What Richard revealed was precisely that, with one addition – he was wearing a lacy red bra that was surprisingly similar to my own. Hmmm, an M&S man, I thought.

Off came his jeans, and Richard stood in front of me in a matching red lacy thong, suspender belt and black stockings.

'All right,' I said, adjusting my impression of him in an instant. A man in lacy underwear? After a couple of years in the business, it was hardly a problem.

But Richard was already explaining: 'Oh my God. I can't believe this! How did I get these on? I've been out drinking all day with some friends, and passed out earlier. My mates must have put these on me and dressed me again while I was asleep.'

'Of course they did,' I said drily. 'Massage?'

Why he felt the need to tell me such a fairy tale was beyond me. Lots of men, I now knew, liked to dress up in women's underwear. His face now as red as what he was wearing, Richard lay on the bed on his front, and I went to work, massaging him, peeling off his bra and thong, sucking, licking, until he came.

As I drove home, longing for the few hours' sleep I'd hopefully squeeze in before I'd be up with the children and off on our Sunday morning ritual to watch Alexander playing rugby as usual, I reflected with a certain grim satisfaction that it might take a little longer, but even those on coke always came in the end.

Alexander scored two tries that morning, and we came home from watching his team romp to victory in celebratory mood. Reeling with tiredness after just three hours' sleep, I put a joint of beef in the oven and whisked up flour, egg and milk to make some Yorkshire puddings. Emily sat at the kitchen table, peeling the potatoes and telling me about her latest singing opportunity with the Kent Youth Choir. They were already working on a concert for Christmas.

'It's going to be beautiful,' she said dreamily.

'I'm sure it will be, darling,' I said, taking the potatoes from her and putting them into water to par-boil. I flashed back to the first time I'd heard her sing a solo in a school concert several years ago – it had been so moving I'd cried. I jolted back to the here and now.

'So will you, Mum?' Emily asked. By the tone of her voice, I could tell this wasn't the first time she'd asked me.

'Sorry, darling,' I said. 'I'm a bit tired. Will I what?'

'Come and see me in the concert? It's a Wednesday night in December, so you'll have to take the night off work.'

December. That was well after my deadline to give up work. I'd be a free woman. How I longed for that time to come. I tried to imagine what it would be like when I could forget all about sex with strangers and simply climb into my own bed each night and sleep, uninterrupted, for hours. It wasn't long now. Only thirteen nights to go. I just had to push through, save what I could, and then it would be over.

'I wouldn't miss it for anything, Emily, you know that. I'll be there.'

The clocks had changed and the evenings started to get dark early.

'Can we have a fireworks party, Mum?' one of the kids asked.

I longed to say yes, but knew it meant I'd have to give up a night's work. Unless I agreed to start late. If I did that, I could do both. I made a snap decision.

'All right, darling, who do you want to come?' I asked.

We invited some of the children's friends, and also Paul, Terry and Jan. Part of me didn't want to, but I knew it was important to keep up the links for the children. And I invited David, wondering if the combination of Paul and David in a room together would cause a few fireworks of a different sort.

The night came, and the bonfire roared at the bottom of our garden. The kids waved their sparklers about, and looking at them all with their cold, rosy faces illuminated by the light from the bonfire, I felt for a moment that we came straight out of a Shirley Hughes children's book. We were everything that was good about middle-class English family life.

Amazingly David and Paul were civil to each other, and I managed to offer Jan, just back from the Caribbean, a sausage politely enough. But as time ticked on, I longed for the guests to leave. I had to get to work. Much as I could have stayed by the bonfire eating sausages all night, I wanted to get my last nights of work over with, and not to have to extend my date for leaving. I could almost taste my freedom from the shackles of the escort world. I didn't want to wait a day longer for it than I had to.

I had known for a while that one of my long-running regular clients was in danger of crossing the invisible line that separates an escort girl from a client by falling in love with me. It wouldn't be the first time it had happened to me. Other clients had grown fond of me – like Tom, the very overweight client who showered me with presents, or Joseph, the single man who wanted to marry me and put my one fictitious child through public school – but no one had ever wanted to leave their wife for me before.

Jim lived in Sussex, where he had a thriving business. He employed at least fifty people and was a millionaire several times over. We had first met the previous year, when he had come to London on business. Since then, he'd been coming to London more and more frequently, and it slowly dawned on me that I was the reason why.

We had fun together, Jim and I. He was an outgoing kind of man, full of zest for life, and that was infectious. He loved musicals, and so did I. Over the past year we'd seen *Les Miserables*, *Joseph and the Amazing Technicolor Dream Coat*, *Elvis*, *Mamma Mia* and many others. An evening with him was hardly work.

He always stayed at the same hotel in Piccadilly, and sometimes, if I could arrange for Sarah to stay over with the children, I'd spend the whole night with him. I'd meet him there in the afternoon, and he'd smoothly sign me in as his wife. We'd have sex, perhaps some champagne, and then get ready for our evening out together. 'What do you fancy seeing?' he'd say. 'You choose something, and ring up and book the tickets. Take my credit card from my wallet to pay.' Jim was good company, the sex was straightforward, and he always paid really well.

Jim had told me he was unhappily married, but I didn't take it too seriously. I had heard this so many times by now that I could be forgiven for thinking it was practically a convention. I thought we had an arrangement that worked for both of us.

But when Jim started coming to London with greater frequency, I couldn't always arrange to stay the night. I knew he was disappointed, but I didn't feel comfortable leaving my children overnight so often. At about the same time, I noticed that every time he booked me, I went home laden with presents. Bottles of perfume, a bunch of spring daffodils, even a fine silver bracelet from Tiffany. It was almost as if he was wooing me.

I hoped against hope I was wrong; that Jim wouldn't go any further, that he wouldn't do or say something that would jeopardise the arrangement we had. It was an arrangement that had worked so well, for so long.

But one evening, as I was halfway through the most delicious bowl of pumpkin risotto at Le Caprice, Jim took my hand in his, looked at me and told me rather firmly that he had something to ask me.

'Elizabeth,' he began. 'I'll come straight to the point.'

Oh God, I thought, putting down my fork. I'd suddenly lost my appetite. I knew it, he'd got the syndrome. Another client who was going to tell me he loved me. Didn't he understand it was a job?

'If I left my wife, could I move in with you?'

Horror-struck, the word was out before I could stop myself: 'No,' I blurted. 'No, most definitely no.'

Jim paled at my vehemence. 'But I love you,' he stammered. 'I thought you felt the same. I want to look after you, marry you, take care of you and your son.' Try six children, I thought grimly.

Belatedly I tried to soften my refusal. 'I'm sorry, Jim. It's a lovely offer. But it simply wouldn't work.'

'Why not?' Jim asked.

A good question, said a small voice in my head. Here I was, blithely turning down a multimillionaire. They don't grow on trees you know, I told myself. Here was someone who could give me everything. I'd never need to work again. And the children weren't really such a problem. I knew that if Jim loved me as he said he did, he'd soon adjust to six stepchildren rather than one. Go on, a little voice in my head said. Say yes. Or at least say you'll think about it.

'I'm sorry, Jim,' I said as gently as I could. 'But the answer is no because I don't love you. The truth is,' I continued slowly, 'I'm in love with someone else.'

After lunch the next day, I was sitting at the kitchen table at home, adding up the takings of the last few nights and putting them in a deposit envelope, when the phone rang.

I picked it up. 'Hello?'

'I just wanted to let you know that I know exactly what you are up to, you little tart,' Jan hissed down the phone.

For a few seconds I was simply too stunned to speak. Then I recovered control of my vocal cords.

'Jan!' I said in amazement. 'Jan!' I repeated, as her words sank deeper into my consciousness. Jan must be my stalker. It had never crossed my mind that it might be Jan. Paul possibly, but not his mother.

'No wonder Paul left. Poor man, his wife a common prostitute. And you with all your high and mighty standards about good manners and a good education. Well, my dear, let's get one thing quite clear. If you so much as lift your little finger in a bid to get Paul to take you back, I'll tell him the whole ugly truth. And by the way, I've got photographs. Is that clear?'

As your vulgar crystal glasses, Jan, I thought.

'Yes,' I replied, momentarily rendered monosyllabic. Photos! I wasn't going to take this from her. But how the hell had she got photos? And of me doing what?

'Poor Paul,' she went on, repeating herself now. 'His wife a hooker.'

'I don't bloody enjoy it, you know,' I exploded. 'And I wouldn't do it unless I absolutely had to. How do you think I've been managing financially?'

'We had no idea – that's why we decided to look into things,' Jan replied smugly.

'If your son wasn't such a dead loss and could help provide for his kids, take some responsibility for them, I wouldn't have to go to such lengths . . .' I tailed off. What was the point? The woman had always disliked me.

'You'll be lucky if you don't lose your kids over this,' Jan said menacingly.

I felt my heart stop. 'Oh, and who's offering to look after them if that happens? You?' I demanded.

Logically, I knew there was no chance Jan would take on six children, she was far too intent on her own pleasures in life; but still. I wasn't feeling very logical right then. I felt sick to my stomach with fear. Imagine if I lost my children because of the very thing that I had done to provide for them, to give them a better life. I could stand anything the world threw at me except losing my kids. If that happened, I knew I would crumble.

'Just don't say you weren't warned,' Jan said darkly. 'Stay away from Paul. Otherwise I'll tell him the truth, and, like I say, I've got evidence. I've had a private investigator tailing you, my dear, and it's been worth every penny.'

The final piece of the jigsaw fell into place. A poisonous silence hung between us. There was nothing else to say.

'Goodbye, Jan,' I said shakily, and replaced the receiver. As I did so, I noticed that my hands were trembling.

I thought for a moment, then picked up the phone again. I needed to sort out this threat hanging over my children, and fast. I needed some legal advice.

The following day I took the train to London after dropping the children at school. I had an appointment with a senior partner in a large firm of solicitors. He specialised in family law.

My stomach was churning in a way it hadn't since my early

jobs. I felt sick with nerves. As I approached the huge glass and steel building that was the solicitors' office, I found myself crossing my fingers. Was I about to hear that there was a possibility I could lose my kids?

Ten minutes later, I was being ushered into the lawyer's office. Bob was in his mid-fifties and clearly a big cheese in the legal world, if his office was anything to go by. A silver-framed photograph of a laughing blonde woman sat on his leather desktop.

'Now,' he began, once we were both settled with cups of coffee in white porcelain mugs. 'How can I help?'

Bob listened intently as I outlined my dilemma, making the odd note on his pad. Then he started to fire questions at me, scribbling down the answers as I gave them.

'You must tell me everything. The whole truth. What does the money go on? Do you spend it on Prada handbags? Do you take drugs? Drink? Who minds the children while you work? Where do the children go to school? Who pays the school fees? The mortgage? What extras do the children have? Who pays for those? Have you ever had a client at home? No? Good. Don't. Who pays for the kids' clothes? What contribution to the outgoings does their father make? Do the grandparents help financially?' And on and on he went until, finally, he dropped his pen and fell silent. Then he put his hands together in a steeple and considered for a moment. His blue eyes were thoughtful.

'So, to recap: you work at night as a prostitute, but all your earnings go to fund your children's life and education.'

'Correct,' I nodded.

'You don't fritter the earnings on a drug or retail habit?'

'No.' I shook my head vehemently.

'Your children have the same reliable babysitters while you work?'

Again I nodded.

'And you pay for everything?'

'Yes.'

'Right. Well, first thing you must do is keep all your receipts – and I mean all – for everything from school fees to dentist's appointments. You need to have everything you can that proves that this – your career – is all about the kids. Just in case.'

'Just in case?' I squeaked nervously. 'In case of what?'

'Well, from what you tell me, your husband is not able to look after the children, so I imagine it's unlikely that he will challenge you for custody of them. But just in case he is foolish enough to do so, you must be able to show that your children are well cared for and that the reason you work is to support them. In other words, you work as a prostitute for the best of all motives. And, also important, we must be able to demonstrate that they are not in any moral danger.'

'Can we do that?' I asked anxiously. I knew they weren't, but how did I prove it to the law?

'Oh yes,' said Bob. 'You work away from home and your children know nothing about what you do. You even store your working equipment off the premises. It would be quite a different matter if you saw clients at home. That would obviously jeopardise their moral well-being. But as things stand, you are a model mother who happens to go to work at night, making sure her children are properly cared for in her absence. Set against that, their father doesn't contribute to their maintenance and sees them intermittently.'

'Paul's not that bad,' I protested. He was, after all, the father of my children.

'No, but if necessary we'll convince the court he is,' Bob said. 'That's the way it works.'

I digested this. I really didn't want an awful legal slanging match with Paul if I could help it. But I'd do anything to keep my kids.

'So you think I'm all right? No one can take my kids away?' I asked.

'I don't think you need to worry,' Bob said. 'I think there is no reason why a judge should recommend that your children should be taken away from you.'

I slumped back in my chair, tension flooding out of my body.

'Thank you so, so much,' I said.

Bob smiled at my relief.

'It's been a pleasure,' he said, handing over his card. 'And call me any time if the situation changes.'

I shook his hand and left.

As I walked out of the building and down the steps, my nerves of earlier were just a memory. My family was safe once more. Paul had no case against me. I knew now that my fears had no basis in reality. If Jan said anything, I'd tell her so.

But as I walked in the direction of the tube, there was still one thought niggling in the corner of my mind. Jan obviously now knew all about my double life, which meant she no longer needed to pay to have me followed by a private investigator. In which case, why had I seen a pale green Peugeot estate pulling away from the kerb opposite the solicitors' firm just minutes ago?

As I bought my ticket and took the escalator down to the platform, I couldn't find a satisfactory answer to this question. I continued to puzzle over it all the way home.

I couldn't let this inconsistency go. I turned it over and over during the next few days, as I made meals and ran children to and from school before going out each night to work, nights only made bearable by the fact that I was now on a countdown of days to go before I stopped.

Once again, a phone call brought the answer. Three days after my visit to London, I got home from dropping the children at school to find my answerphone beeping. I was feeling rather buoyant as my escort days were about to be consigned to the dustbin. I pressed the button to find it was a message from my friend Viv asking me to call her urgently.

Viv worked for an American law firm in London, and I'd known her for over ten years. She had known I was an escort girl almost from the outset, and had helped me process my accounts each year – I had no intention of falling foul of the tax man. Coincidentally, she was also a good friend of David. Wondering what could be so urgent, I rang her back.

'Oh God,' she groaned. 'You are simply going to kill me.'

'Why? What have you done?' I asked. I couldn't imagine.

'I saw David at the train station this morning,' she began.

For no good reason, I shivered.

'We got chatting. I wouldn't have told him, but he said he already knew. He said he knew what you were up to, and that he was fine about it.'

My blood was slowly turning to ice. 'What did you say?' I whispered.

'I'm so, so sorry,' Viv stammered. I could tell how upset she was by the break in her voice.

'It's okay, Viv, but what did you say?' I both dreaded knowing and wanted to hear it as quickly as possible.

Viv sighed. I could tell that, metaphorically at least, she had her head in her hands. Then she said it all in a rush: 'I said, thank goodness for that, after all, prostitution isn't so bad, is it?'

'And what did David say?' I hardly dared to ask.

'He just went white. And I knew then that he had been bluffing. He hadn't known, after all.'

I closed my eyes and leaned my head against the cool wood of the kitchen table as Viv's repeated apologies rang in my ears.

'Don't worry, Viv,' I reassured her wearily. 'It's not your fault.'

And I knew that it wasn't. It was mine for not telling David earlier; it was mine for doing it in the first place. The fault, the blame, lay entirely with me.

Suddenly, something fell into place in my mind. The pale green Peugeot hadn't been Jan's private detective. I had had not one, but two private investigators looking into my life. The first had been authorised by Jan. The second, in a pale green Peugeot, had been working for a client I now very much suspected was a man called David.

I said goodbye to Viv and wondered how I felt. The worst had happened. David had found me out. As a liar and as a call girl. I looked around me, at the children's paintings stuck on the walls, at the pinboard in the corner reminding me of all the things I had to do. Well, my world hadn't collapsed. Technically, everything was still here.

I probed deeper. Strangely, a part of me was relieved. I was so tired of all the lies. Now David knew the truth, and however bad that was, at least it meant no more lying to the man I loved. But the relief was tinted with a gnawing fear. What did David think of me? Could he still love me? Or would he leave me?

Tired, so tired, I rested my head once again on the kitchen table while I considered this possibility of David leaving me. I knew now that everything in life carried a price. Would this be the price I had to pay for saving my family? I found the cool, grainy wood against my forehead oddly soothing. I wished I could go to sleep for a long time and wake up refreshed, as I hadn't felt for a while, no longer working, to find out that my kids were all happy and well and that David still loved me.

The door bell roused me out of a semi-slumber. I went to answer it. I knew who it would be; I was just surprised he had taken so long to get here.

'David,' I said.

He came straight to the point. 'Why didn't you tell me?' he asked, shaking his head in disbelief.

'If I'd known you at the beginning like I know you now, I probably would have,' I said quietly. 'But I didn't know you well enough at first. And then, when I did – well, I loved you. And . . . I didn't want to lose you. It suddenly seemed too big a risk to take.'

David came in, and, his eyes filled with a mixture of sadness and anger, he put his arms round me. Somehow, we were kissing. Hand in hand we made our way upstairs, and David was pushing me back on the bed, lying me down, peeling off my clothes; we were making love, still, despite it all, unable to keep our hands off each other. A small flame of hope flared. Perhaps he did understand. Perhaps he wouldn't leave me, after all.

Afterwards, we lay in silence. I could feel a chill descending on my naked skin. David sat up and started to get dressed. He reached into his jacket pocket and pulled something out.

'For you,' he said, handing me a folded piece of paper. I opened it slowly. It was a cheque for three hundred pounds.

'For the sex,' he said, at last revealing his icy rage.

'Goodbye, "Elizabeth",' he said, mocking me with my working name.

I said nothing.

I listened to his fading footsteps, as if as long as I could still hear them there was hope he would change his mind, that he would turn round, come back upstairs, take me in his arms, tell me he still loved me. Tell me he'd just been so angry at the thought of all those other men touching me, and that if I stopped work that very moment it would all be all right.

Instead, I heard the latch turn and click a few seconds later as he shut the door behind him.

The house fell into a deep silence. I don't know how long I lay there, exhausted in every way, too tired and drained to move. But eventually, the clock told me it was nearly three. I had to get up. I had to collect the children from school, pick up the younger ones from the childminder, cook something for tea, help with homework, bath them and wash everyone's hair before getting myself ready for work. I wriggled my toes experimentally, almost surprised to see them move to order. Physically, everything was still working. It was back on to the treadmill for me. The hamster wheel of life. There was simply no time for my heart to be broken.

Woodenly, I swung my legs to the floor and sat up, and life ground relentlessly on.

I was on automatic that afternoon. I did all the things I was meant to do: I picked up the kids, laughed at their jokes, asked them questions about their day, took them home, cooked them their tea, dropped Charlotte at riding and Emily at choir practice. Later everyone did their homework, and then it was bathtime for the little ones.

Finally, with the younger ones in their brushed-cotton pyjamas, and tucked up in bed, I set off for work with lead in my soul. My heart no longer missed a beat when I reminded myself that I had less than one week of work left before I stopped for good. There was no skip in my step at my impending freedom.

My eyes were gritty from lack of sleep. but I worked through my bookings like a robot. The clients, a series of one-offs, didn't seem to notice anything amiss, so I must have performed my work well enough. It had become second nature to me to give blow jobs and hand jobs, to fuck, to lick, to flatter; to feign interest in a stranger's life, to give compliments, to undo flies and extract a hardening cock with one well-manicured hand before enclosing it with my lipsticked mouth.

Never had I hated my work as I did that night. In between jobs, as I drove from Dartford to Tunbridge Wells, then to Reigate and back to Dartford, delivering my service, collecting the cash, I saw only how low I had fallen. I had suffered so much degradation, had so many men spit on me and call me a whore. And now I had lost the man I loved. It hurt so much that I wondered if I was ill.

Finally, exhaustedly, I climbed into my car for the last time that night. My next stop was home. It was an easy drive, straight along the M3 until my junction and then a fifteen-minute meander. I felt very tired, more than ever before. I took a sip of a takeaway coffee I'd bought hours ago and long gone cold, hoping it would help, and started the engine. Hang on, I told myself. Hang on. Not long now.

I turned on the radio and told myself about the bath and the hot cup of tea I'd make myself when I got home. No point going to bed – it was already five in the morning. By the time I got home it would be nearly six. The children got up at seven. I knew from experience that it was worse to go to bed for a bare hour's sleep than to stay awake until after the children were at school. I fantasised instead about how I would come back from the school run, ignore the mess of breakfast in the kitchen, climb the stairs, take off my clothes and fall into bed, huddling the duvet all round me. I could see myself as if I were watching someone else: that person who looked so like me was snuggling their head down into the pillow, limbs cosy under the duvet, finally giving into their tiredness and closing their eyes . . .

Crash. The world went black.

I opened my eyes slowly. My head hurt. I frowned, and looked around, trying to absorb my surroundings. There was a large expanse of empty, grey road to my left. I turned my head the other way. There was a large expanse of empty, grey road to my right. I looked ahead, and with a surge of adrenaline coursing through me, I understood.

I had fallen asleep at the wheel. I had fallen asleep at the wheel on the way home and crashed into the central reservation.

Still sitting in the driver's seat, my seat belt on, I looked at what I could see of the car now. Amazingly, from the driver's perspective, it looked as if there was barely a dent. Thank God for the client in the car dealership, instrumental in my having this new 4×4. I felt sure I would have died in my old car. I turned the key experimentally to find it started at first go. Hands shaking as I clung on to the wheel, I gently eased the car off the central reservation and pulled out into the empty motorway. I moved over to the slow lane and drove at a steady fifty. I didn't dare go faster. I knew I was having some kind of reaction. My whole body was stiff with a flood of emotions – adrenalin, fear, shock, all mixed with the now perpetual exhaustion.

Hold it together, I told myself. Hold it together.

As the car hummed along in the slow lane, I found I was shaking my head gently in disbelief. The last month had been one of the most horrific of my life. Well, I thought, indicating carefully to exit the motorway, double-checking in my rear mirror that the road was clear, that was it. That was absolutely it. I was stopping work. Not next week as I'd planned, but right now. No more prevarication. I'd nearly died, for God's sake. How the hell would that have helped my children? How much more of a wake-up call did I need? I was absolutely exhausted, I was risking my life, I simply had to stop.

I felt my body relax a little more into the seat, and I knew beyond doubt that I had made the right decision. My days as an escort girl were behind me. It might have had its terrible moments, I might be half dead with exhaustion, but I had to admit that I had accomplished what I'd set out to do. I'd paid off our debts and my home was my own. All right, so my marriage had broken up and my children had partially lost their father, but I felt certain that would have happened anyway. What my children had gained as a result of my working was stability in their lives in every other way: same schools, same friends, and a loving, constant mother.

I thought of my children and my heart swelled. They'd all come on so much in the last few years. Emily's singing had gone from strength to strength; Alice was popular and working hard; Alexander wasn't exactly academic, but he was my five-star rugby player, and Charlotte was simply pony mad; Victoria, dear Victoria, so gutsy, was overcoming her difficulties and refusing to be left out of any childhood adventure; and last but not least, Jack, my noisy, boisterous Lego-obsessed Jack, so energetic, so loving, and fast leaving his babyhood behind.

I smiled as I thought about them all – my reasons for living, my reasons for doing what I'd done. I was on my way home to them now, and I wasn't going to be rushing away ever again. I was through with all that. It was over.

I've given up! The thought rose in me like the sun. The notion that I could put my suspender years behind me made me want to cheer. And, I told myself, as if I didn't quite believe it, I really could do it – we had enough in the bank to keep us going until I found a new way to pay for our lives. So what if I was stopping six nights earlier than I'd planned. We still had a good six months' grace before I needed to start earning again.

I would have to spend the first few weeks of that time sleeping, resting, recovering. But even as I thought this, I felt a small surge of my natural energy return. I would be all right. As I shed my exhaustion, I could embark on laying the groundwork for my future source of income. And I had a small germ of an idea about what that source of income might be.

It was six forty-five in the morning and I was nearly home. The sun was fully up now. It was going to be one of the kind of days that Britain does best – a clear, crisp, late-autumnal day. The sky was an even, brilliant shade of blue. As I turned the car into my street, I felt a flowering of hope. My children were happy and well, and my future lay ahead of me.

And David? I forced myself to think of him, however much it

hurt. It was an instinct I couldn't resist, like the continual probing of a sore tooth. I knew I'd never love like that again. He was no storybook hero, but my real, flesh-and-blood love. I could only hope that he'd forgive me. Perhaps, given time, he would come to understand why I had made the choice I had. That every lie I had told him had been told only to serve that primary, essential purpose – to enable me to earn the money I needed for my family to survive.

I pulled up outside my house and switched off the engine. It seemed like I had left for work a lifetime ago. So much had happened, and yet, in reality, hadn't it all been happening for far longer than just the last few hours? I took off my seat belt, opened the car door and shut it quietly behind me. The children were probably still asleep. I let myself in and stood for a moment, listening.

The house was silent. I took off my coat and began to climb the stairs. I paused at the top for a moment, outside the first door, which led to Emily and Alice's room. Then, quietly, I pushed the handle down and went in.

Emily and Alice were both fast asleep. Emily lay tucked up under her duvet, as neat in sleep as in life, her brown hair spreading on the pillow, while Alice had kicked the duvet off and had her arms thrown wide. Around her, her possessions lay scattered in a careless trail from cupboard to bed and back again. At least three pairs of trousers lay strewn across the floor, and her dressing table was littered with half-open pots and tubes. Her face looked too absurdly young and perfect to need any of their contents.

Resisting the urge to kiss my two eldest daughters, I tiptoed out again, nearly falling over Emily's music stand, and went into the next room.

Charlotte and Victoria. These were my little girls. Charlotte, pony mad, and Victoria, my sweet, courageous tomboy. Raking the room with my eyes, I realised that their room, too, could do with a jolly good tidy. Toys were scattered everywhere, a couple of books lay on the floor, and a skateboard that should have been in the hall sat by Victoria's bed.

I went back out into the corridor and along to Alexander and Jack's room. Typical boys' room, I thought, stifling a giggle. Socks lay abandoned like islands in the sea; Jack, forever doing Lego, had piled some red and yellow bricks by the bookcase. The cupboard doors were both open, and clothes hung drunkenly, half off their hangers. Alexander, I noticed, had his beloved England rugby shirt on top of his pyjamas. Posters of his rugby heroes were stuck up on the wall.

I walked out again, closing the door quietly behind me. The sun was up now, pouring into the windows. It was for these wonderful children, I thought, as I made my way to my own room to change out of my work clothes for the last time, that I had done what I had done. For these six individual, talented children, I had given my all. I had lived through some terrible experiences and lost the man I loved in the process, but still, I thought as I pulled on my jeans, it had been worth it. They were happy, they were stable, they were progressing in the world; they were just embarking on life, and very little had yet marred it for them. It meant everything to me to see them realising their promise, and I knew they had every hope of achieving all their dreams. All of them pursued their hobbies, confident enough to believe they could have a good stab at them. All of them knew why it was important to work at school, and every one of them had manners and a kindness to be proud of. As I descended the stairs again, heading to the kitchen for a cup of tea, I felt so proud of my children for the valuable human beings that they were.

Then, for a moment, a different image came into my mind. Of children disrupted by the loss of their father, their home, their schools, their schoolfriends, all at once; children with no way of pursuing the hobbies that contributed to their self-esteem; children taken from everything they knew and loved, dumped, without warning, in an alien world. Would those children have grown up to be as confident, as achieving, as steady as the ones sleeping in their beds upstairs?

I poured the boiling water on to the tea bag and crossed to the fridge to add some milk. Of course I had no way of knowing for sure. I had taken one road and would never know the consequences of the other that I had turned away from. But my instinct as their mother told me that, nearly three years on from losing everything that made their lives stable, they would very possibly have been at a different place now.

I sipped my tea, relaxing as it spread its warm tentacles through me, and nodded to myself, riding a wave of certainty. I knew beyond reasonable doubt that I had done the right thing, in spite of the personal price I had had to pay. I shied away from asking myself what mark the experience had left on me. Suffice it to say that I had survived.

I glanced up at the kitchen clock. Seven-fifteen. It was time for me to wake the children. It was a school morning, after all, even if it felt to me like Christmas Day and my birthday all rolled into one. I put my cup down, stood up and stretched. It was early days, I reflected, but I felt quite all right in myself.

I turned towards the kitchen door, and, as I did so, a flash of movement caught my eye through the kitchen window. It looked like a man was coming up the front path. Blinking back the tiredness, I went to the front door and opened it.

David. He stood in front of me, silent. But his arms were held wide, as if he wanted me to fall into them. And he was smiling at me.